The Age of Storms: John Reynolds' Financial Struggle is a work of fiction. Names, characters, places, and incidents either are products of the author's imagination or are used fictitiously. Any resemblance to actual persons, living or dead, or actual events is purely coincidental.

Copyright © 2024 Harrison.H.

All rights reserved.

No part of this book may be reproduced, distributed, or transmitted in any form or by any means without the prior written permission of the publisher, except in the case of brief quotations in reviews and certain non-commercial uses permitted by copyright law.

First Edition 2024.

ISBN: 9798345798249

"History never repeats itself exactly, but stories always unfold in similar ways. What remains eternal and unchanging is human nature."

THE AGE OF STORMS: JOHN REYNOLDS'
FINANCIAL STRUGGLE

CHAPTER 1

DESERT FLAMES 1990

The Shadow of War

In 1990, tensions were escalating in the Middle East. The region's vast oil reserves, the lifeblood of the global economy, made it a focal point for international conflict.

Iraq had just emerged from a long and bloody war with Iran in the 1980s and was in a dire economic situation. The war had depleted its treasury, crippled its domestic economy, and left millions homeless and without livelihoods. Iraqi leader Saddam Hussein, eager to restore his nation's power, desperately sought solutions to quickly revive the economy. His attention soon turned to neighboring Kuwait.

Kuwait, though small in size, possessed abundant oil reserves. Saddam believed that Kuwait's oil was crucial for Iraq's economic recovery. Relations between Iraq and Kuwait were deteriorating due to long-standing border disputes, including disagreements over Warba Island and the Rumaila oil field, as well as Kuwait's oil market strategies. Iraq accused Kuwait of overproducing oil, driving down global prices and thereby worsening Iraq's economic hardship, as the country was heavily reliant on oil revenue. Kuwait maintained that it was merely adjusting production according to market demand and dismissed Iraq's accusations as unreasonable pressure.

Further fueling the antagonism were Iraq's claims of sovereignty over Kuwaiti oil fields. Saddam asserted that Kuwait was not only "stealing" Iraqi oil but also selling it below market value, deliberately depressing global prices and directly harming Iraq's interests. These disputes not only created tension in the Middle East but also drew significant international attention. The United Nations condemned Iraq's threats and called for a peaceful resolution to the conflict. Meanwhile, the United States deployed troops to the region to protect Saudi Arabia and put pressure on Iraq, attempting to deter further escalation.

In July, New York City sweltered in suffocating humidity, a stark contrast to the frigid air conditioning on the Moorman Investment Group's trading floor. Each trader's desk held a bulky computer terminal, and the occasional screech of a dial-up modem pierced the air like an unstable connection to the pulse of the financial world. In this era, before personal computers were ubiquitous, traders still tracked market trends manually. The walls were lined with massive sheets of paper filled with meticulously hand-drawn candlestick charts, each line capturing the volatile swings in oil prices.

Under the pale glow of fluorescent lights, the atmosphere mirrored the uncertainty of the times. Traders hunched over stacks of paper reports, rapidly calculating daily market data. Every so often, someone would stand abruptly, muttering, "The price changed again!" Frantic hands scribbled updates on sprawling charts, while voices barked into outdated phones. The incessant ringing of phones, like shrill sirens, mingled with anxious voices echoing across the confined space, creating a chaotic symphony of sound.

"Brent crude has hit another high! Thirty dollars! My God, it's thirty dollars!" a trader shouted, his voice carrying a blend of alarm and disbelief.

John Reynolds stood at his desk, his grip instinctively tightening around his coffee mug. The bitter liquid trembled as his hand shook slightly, on the verge of spilling. His heart pounded in his chest, matching the frantic rhythm of the flickering numbers on his monitor and the volatile charts surrounding him. The cacophony of ringing phones and hurried footsteps filled his ears, amplifying the tension in the room.

The chaos of the trading floor weighed heavily on John. The constantly shifting numbers on the screen seemed to mock his inexperience, each fluctuation a reminder of his tenuous grasp on this fast-paced world. His heartbeat quickened, mirroring the erratic movements on the terminal. He had envisioned himself confidently navigating the hallowed halls of Wall Street, a model of rationality and composure. But reality was far more brutal, pressing down on him with an almost physical force.

"I thought I could handle these numbers easily," he murmured, "but now, even my basic judgment is faltering." He recalled scenes from his college lectures, where he had listened with passion to professors explaining financial markets, filled with hope for a brilliant future. Now, those idealized visions felt hollow against the chaos of the trading room.

"Is this Wall Street?" he wondered, trying to quell a rising sense of unease.

Fresh out of the University of New England, he had entered this skyscraper filled with ambition, determined to conquer the financial world. But the reality before him was a far cry from the rational, orderly world he had envisioned. Panic, anxiety, greed—these emotions clung to the air, thick and almost suffocating, challenging every ideal he had brought with him.

Suddenly, a CNN news broadcast took over the giant screen in the trading room. The grainy image, typical of 1990s television, clearly showed Iraqi tanks advancing like a black torrent, churning up desert sands. The soldiers' grim expressions, intensified by the low resolution, pointed to the inevitable—the outbreak of war. The coarse footage heightened the sense of dread, as if the shadow of the distant battlefield had fallen over the entire room.

"Everyone," a calm voice came from behind John. It was Richard Harkins. "Capital is flowing out of stocks and into safe-haven assets like gold and bonds. It looks like the market's fears of war are hitting full force." Richard, a composed man with over thirty years of experience on Wall Street, had faced many market crises before; his calm demeanor was a testament to his expertise.

John turned and saw his mentor, the senior investment manager at Moorman Investment Group, gazing intently at the screen. Richard was the one person John could rely on in this unfamiliar environment.

"John," Richard's eyes met his, "what do you think this war will do to the oil market?"

John hesitated, his mind racing through the financial models and theories he had learned in college. But he quickly realized that textbook knowledge paled in comparison to the real-world uncertainty he now faced.

"I… I'm not sure," John replied, hesitant. "But if war breaks out, oil supplies will definitely be disrupted, and prices could keep climbing."

"Correct," Richard nodded. "But the question is, how high will prices go? How long will the war last? These are the unknowns. We need to make rational judgments based on how the market reacts."

John nodded, though he only half understood. His eyes drifted back to the screen, where the CNN anchor was reporting on the latest developments: Iraqi troops were closing in on the Kuwaiti border. War seemed imminent.

"Thirty-two dollars! My God!" A trader's startled shout snapped John out of his thoughts.

As the pressure from outside intensified, John felt his vulnerability laid bare. Every time the phone rang, his hand gripped his coffee cup tighter, his palms slick with sweat. He couldn't help but think, "Can I handle this pressure?" Surrounded by seasoned traders, he felt like a small boat being tossed around in a storm, the waves threatening to engulf him. He began to question his own ability. "Am I just an outsider here? Will I find my place in this industry?" This gnawing doubt clouded his mind, overwhelming him. Each time he saw his colleagues calmly handling the chaos, his own insecurity grew. "They're all so confident, and I'm just lost, like a child." This self-doubt left him feeling increasingly isolated.

John took a deep breath, forcing himself to calm down. He knew he had to learn quickly, to adapt to this environment brimming with risk and uncertainty. This wasn't just a war—it was a global financial battleground, and he, a novice in the world of finance, had already been thrust into the middle of this invisible conflict.

The Surge in Oil Prices

On August 2, as Iraq invaded Kuwait, war officially erupted, and the global markets were struck as if a massive stone had been thrown into a still pond, stirring waves of shock and turbulence. Simultaneously, British Prime Minister Margaret Thatcher and U.S. President George H.W. Bush held a joint press conference in Aspen, Colorado, publicly condemning Iraq's invasion of Kuwait. Both leaders emphasized their refusal to tolerate Saddam Hussein's aggression, calling on the international community to unite in response to this crisis.

As news of the invasion spread, the financial world held its breath, anticipating the economic aftershocks that could ripple globally. The trading floor at Moorman Investment Group was a cacophony of noise. Keyboards clicked, phones rang, and traders shouted, their voices merging into a deafening roar. Anxiety and unease etched every face as crude oil prices surged like a wild stallion. Brent crude had rocketed from $30 to nearly $40 in just a few days.

John felt swept away by a financial tsunami, overwhelmed by the flood of information and data. He stared intently at his computer screen, desperately searching for patterns in the chaotic numbers and charts. But it was futile. The futures market remained an alien jungle, dense with unknowns and fraught with danger.

Tension crackled in the air, thick with oppressive pressure. Phones rang incessantly, each ring signaling another potential crisis. Traders paced back and forth, the clatter of heels and keyboard clicks blending into an unsettling rhythm. Some barked into their phones, their voices edged with anxiety and frustration, while others cursed under their breath, slamming down receivers or pounding their desks.

Behind John, a young trader suddenly shoved back his chair, the wheels screeching against the floor. "No, impossible!" he yelled into the phone. "We can't sell at this price!" His hands clenched in his hair, and his face twisted in despair.

In stark contrast to the surrounding chaos, John's world seemed to narrow. He fixated on his computer screen, the flickering numbers a dense fog he couldn't penetrate, his heart pounding in his chest. Determined to focus, he threw himself into the data analysis. His fingers flew across the keyboard, each keystroke amplified in his ears, a sharp counterpoint to the surrounding noise.

Just as John was immersing himself in the data, the glass door to the trading room swung open, and a woman in a tailored suit strode in with a confident air. All eyes turned to the newcomer—Katherine Morgan, a rising star and senior partner at Moorman Investment Group. Known for her sharp decision-making and keen market instincts, she was a formidable force in the male-dominated world of Wall Street.

"Everyone, we have a strategy meeting at ten," Katherine announced, her calm voice carrying an air of unquestionable authority. Her gaze swept across the room before landing on John. "John, are your figures ready?"

A surge of pressure hit John, but he knew he couldn't afford to falter. "Almost finished, Katherine," he replied, his fingers flying across the keyboard as he tried to compile all the data into a report before the meeting.

Katherine nodded, her eyes scanning the documents on her desk with cool composure. Every movement exuded efficiency and professionalism. "The data from the oil futures market is crucial; we can't afford any mistakes. This is your first major project, John. Don't be nervous—just focus on the bigger picture."

As she left, John couldn't help but admire her. Katherine's decisiveness and composure intimidated him, but it also drove home the point that knowledge alone wasn't enough in this cutthroat world; decisive action was essential.

Despite his eagerness to fit in, John still felt like an outsider. During lunch breaks, he would often overhear his colleagues discussing their successful trades and investment strategies, while he remained a silent observer, filled with a mix of envy and unease. He wanted to join the conversations, but he was afraid his opinions would be dismissed or ridiculed.

"What if I say something wrong? Will they look down on me?" This worry plagued him, making him even more reserved within the team. He began to doubt his abilities, even questioning his career choice.

"John," his mentor Richard Harkins' voice cut through his thoughts. "The oil futures market is critical right now. You need to learn to read it, analyze it, and predict it." Richard, a veteran of Wall Street's battles for over three decades, maintained his usual composure, his gaze sharp as an eagle's, as if he could see through the market's every secret.

John tried to steady himself, focusing on the futures market, but the screen was a jumble of contract information—different expiration dates, fluctuating prices, and varying volumes—and it was overwhelming.

"The futures market is much more volatile than the spot market," Richard said, pointing at a line on the screen. "See, this is the price trend of near-month crude oil futures. It reflects the market's expectations for oil prices in the coming months."

John followed Richard's finger. He saw a line that looked like a roller coaster, with peaks and troughs far surpassing the fluctuations of the spot price.

"Why does the futures price fluctuate so dramatically?" John asked, puzzled.

"Because the participants in the futures market are more diverse," Richard explained. "Besides oil producers and consumers who need physical delivery, there are also many speculators. They use leverage to amplify both their gains and their risks, chasing every market fluctuation."

John nodded, a flicker of recognition crossing his face. He remembered his university lessons on the futures market: futures contracts allowed traders to buy or sell a commodity at a predetermined price on a future date. Now, with the outbreak of war, concerns about future oil supplies had intensified, causing futures prices to soar.

"Those speculators holding oil futures contracts," Richard continued, "are like people sitting on the crater of a volcano. They could be swallowed by the market's lava at any moment."

John could almost picture the anxious faces of those speculators—some desperately selling their contracts to secure profits, while others frantically bought in hopes of further price increases that could bring them enormous wealth.

"In the futures market," Richard said gravely, "risk and return are always proportional. You have to learn to manage risk to survive in this market."

John nodded, understanding the profound meaning in Richard's words. The futures market held both allure and danger; it could make a fortune overnight or wipe someone out just as quickly.

"John," Richard said, patting him on the shoulder, "observe the market changes closely, and try to understand the logic behind the data. This war is both a challenge and an opportunity for you."

John asked, "Richard, what qualities do you think a successful investor should have?"

Richard paused, thinking for a moment. "Well," he said, "I think it takes a few things: a sharp eye for spotting opportunities, for one; and the ability to think clearly and make sound decisions, even under pressure. You have to be decisive, too, and able to act quickly when you see a chance. And maybe most importantly," he added, "you need a strong mind to handle the risks and the stress."

John nodded, deeply impressed by Richard's words. He realized that he still had much to learn and needed to keep improving if he ever wanted to become a true investment master.

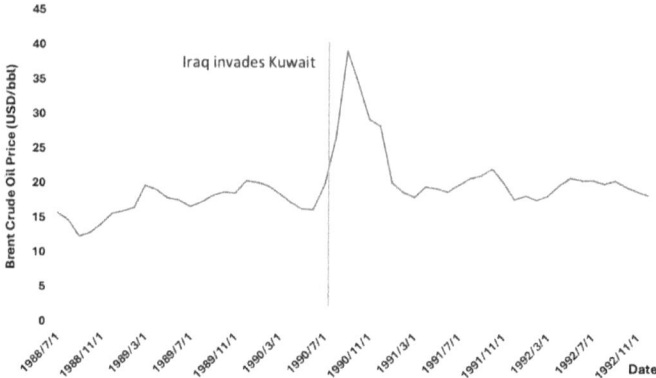

The chart shows the fluctuation of Brent crude oil prices from 1988 to 1992, with the sharp spike in prices following Iraq's invasion of Kuwait in 1990 being particularly notable. This event had a profound impact on the global economy and financial markets, becoming one of the most significant oil price shocks in history.
Source of data: U.S. Energy Information Administration (EIA).

The Challenge of a Novice

John felt like a small boat adrift in the stormy sea of finance. Everyone else in the trading room seemed like seasoned sailors, navigating the tempest with calm confidence, while he clung to the railing, struggling to avoid being swept away by the relentless waves. He watched the rapidly changing numbers and looming deadlines on the contracts. A wave of doubt washed over him. Did he truly belong in this world?

"John," the voice of his mentor, Richard Harkins, brought him back from his thoughts. Richard stood beside him, his gaze steady and encouraging. "Don't worry; it's normal to feel overwhelmed in this kind of situation. Take it slow; you'll learn a lot."

Richard's presence was like a beacon, guiding John through this unfamiliar financial jungle. Taking a deep breath, John tried to calm his nerves and followed Richard to a large conference table.

"We're conducting an emergency risk assessment," Richard said, gesturing for him to sit down. "This is a good learning opportunity for you."

Ten people were already seated around the table, the atmosphere thick with tension. John recognized some of the company's partners and senior executives among them. Their faces were etched with worry, and the room was filled with the rustling of papers as they nervously flipped through their documents.

"Everyone," began Williams, the senior partner, his voice low and steady, "the surge in oil prices has exceeded our expectations. The situation is critical. We need to quickly re-evaluate the risk exposure of all our portfolios, especially the 'Energy Pioneer' fund and the Middle Eastern real estate projects, as these are most affected by oil price volatility."

"We must immediately reduce our holdings in oil-related stocks," Katherine stated, her voice calm and professional, radiating an air of decisiveness. She tapped her finger on the table, her gaze sweeping across the room. "At the same time, we should buy call options on oil futures to hedge against the risk of rising prices. This will allow us to minimize our exposure and maintain flexibility. As for interest rate swaps, we should consider those to mitigate any sudden market fluctuations."

Her tone was devoid of emotion, as if the war and market turmoil were merely a mathematical equation to be solved. Her professionalism and composure impressed John, yet also intimidated him. He could hardly imagine himself staying so calm in such a situation.

"I agree," Steve, a senior investment manager, nodded. "We can't put all our eggs in one basket. As oil prices continue to soar, we need to take more hedging measures to protect our capital. The airline and automotive sectors are particularly vulnerable to rising oil prices, so I recommend reducing our exposure to those immediately."

Steve was the quintessential Wall Street elite—a graduate of a prestigious university with sharp data analysis skills and a keen market sense. He favored high-risk, high-reward investment strategies, seeing market crises as opportunities rather than setbacks. His approach contrasted sharply with that of more conservative investors; he always trusted his judgment and believed that bold action in times of crisis was the key to success.

John sat quietly, observing these seasoned investors. He was still processing the complex discussion, much of the terminology and strategies being unfamiliar to him. But he tried to remain calm, absorbing every detail of the tense meeting. He admired their composure; despite the chaos outside, they remained rational and methodical.

"John," Williams suddenly interrupted the discussion, calling his name. All eyes turned to him, and his heart pounded as his palms grew damp with sweat.

"What are your thoughts on this, John? Let's hear your analysis."

John took a deep breath, his eyes darting around the room before settling on Richard, seeking reassurance. His voice wavered slightly. "I… I think… the price of oil… will continue to rise for a while, but… it should eventually return… to a more reasonable level."

He paused, his mind racing, but he knew he had to continue. "Because… with the multinational coalition involved, the military operation… shouldn't last too long." He swallowed, forcing himself to slow down. "Once oil supply… recovers, the price… will likely fall. Investor panic… should also subside."

He finished, stealing a glance at Richard, still unsure of himself. Though his analysis wasn't perfect, at least he had managed to express his thoughts.

Williams, seated at the conference table, nodded in agreement. "Well said, John. You can see the long-term market trends, which are insightful." He paused, his gaze sweeping across the room, his expression turning serious. "But we must also prepare for the worst. Oil prices could continue to rise, perhaps even exceeding $50 a barrel. If that happens, the global economy will face an unprecedented shock."

"$50?" John's heart tightened. He couldn't imagine the devastation such a high oil price would wreak on the world. He took a quiet breath, trying to quell his rising anxiety.

"Indeed," Katherine picked up where William left

off. "Steve, your analysis was spot on. Airlines and automakers are the most directly affected by rising oil prices. We need to monitor their stock prices closely and adjust our investment strategies accordingly."

Steve adjusted his glasses, his lips tightening slightly. "But I think John's view is overly optimistic. He lacks experience and hasn't weathered a real market crisis."

Steve's words cut like a knife, slicing through John's pride. His cheeks burned, and his heart raced as if he were being scrutinized and judged. He lowered his head, trying to ignore Steve's remark, but his anxiety intensified.

Richard interjected, "Steve, don't be so quick to dismiss the young man's perspective. While John's analysis may have its shortcomings, his overall direction is correct." He turned to John, offering encouragement. "John, continue learning and constantly improving your analytical skills. Don't be afraid to make mistakes—learning from them is the fastest way to grow."

The meeting progressed, the discussion growing more intense. As it concluded, Williams called John back. "John, stay for a moment." He gestured for John to sit, placing a report in front of him.

"This crisis is more complex than you think, John. It's not just about oil prices; there are geopolitics, supply chain disruptions, and more," Williams's voice was low and sincere. "You need to learn to see risk from a holistic perspective and make decisions under pressure."

John nodded, suppressing his nervousness to show that he was listening.

"I'm going to give you a more central role in our decision-making process," Williams continued. "You'll be working with Richard, assisting him in adjusting our key investment portfolios. This is about understanding the bigger picture, seeing all the factors involved, and being able to act decisively when it matters."

Williams paused, then said softly, "I believe you can do it, but you must remain vigilant. The market won't give you a second chance."

John's heart pounded. He understood this was more than just guidance; it was a significant test. He looked at Williams, determined to prove himself.

"I understand, Mr. Williams," he replied, his voice firm. "I'll give it my all and won't let you down."

Williams nodded and turned to leave. John watched him go, his heart filled with determination.

Crisis Decisions

In the trading room of Moorman Investment Group, everyone's attention was involuntarily drawn to the latest CNN news broadcast. **"This is Global News with a special live report. We bring you today's most explosive headlines,"** the anchor's voice echoed through the room. **"As the Gulf conflict escalates, global tensions are running high. Oil prices are surging, and nations around the world are on edge."**

The screen shifted to Helsinki, Finland, where a somber reporter spoke in a low, urgent tone: **"Today, on September 9, 1990, Soviet President Gorbachev and U.S. President Bush held a historic meeting. Afterward, both leaders issued a joint statement, strongly condemning Iraq's invasion of Kuwait and calling for Iraq's unconditional withdrawal."**

As the news finished, the tension in the trading

room grew heavier. Phones rang in quick succession; rapid conversations and the sound of keyboards filled the air. Traders moved swiftly, their expressions tense. Low curses and the rustle of papers intertwined with trading orders, creating a dense backdrop of noise. John, assigned to work beside Richard, handled basic data analysis and trading instructions. Though it was his first job, the pressure around him felt like an invisible weight on his shoulders, leaving him no room to make a single mistake.

"John," Katherine approached them, her voice urgent, "Mr. Williams wants us to adjust the 'Energy Pioneer' fund's portfolio immediately. How's your data analysis coming along?" John felt a surge of nervousness but knew he had to respond quickly.

"Katherine, I'm analyzing it right now," John replied, swiftly presenting the compiled data to her. "Currently, it appears that airline and some automotive stocks have the highest risk exposure."

Katherine scanned the data, her brow furrowing slightly. Then, a satisfied smile spread across her face. "Excellent work, John. Your analysis aligns with my assessment. I believe we should reduce our holdings in those stocks immediately and increase our position in oil companies to hedge against the rising oil prices."

"I agree," Richard concurred. "But we also need to consider other risk factors, such as the companies' cash flow, debt levels, and management's ability to respond to this crisis."

"Richard's right," Katherine added. "Especially those companies with high debt levels. If oil prices continue to rise, their capital chains could break."

"I understand," John nodded earnestly, realizing the need for a more comprehensive analysis.

Katherine glanced at the clock, her voice edged with anxiety. "Time is of the essence. We need to make decisions swiftly. John, compile this analysis into a report and bring it to me."

"Of course," John responded, his fingers flying across the keyboard.

As Katherine turned to leave, Richard gave John's shoulder a reassuring pat. "Don't worry; you're doing well. In times of crisis, we need to stay calm, react quickly, and pay attention to detail."

John met Richard's gaze with gratitude, recognizing the importance of his guidance and encouragement.

"John," Richard paused, a hint of challenge in his voice, "how do you think this crisis differs from the oil crisis of the 1980s?"

John furrowed his brow, contemplating the question before responding, "This crisis is far larger in scale, and the global markets are more interconnected. Even minor fluctuations can trigger chain reactions that impact the entire world's economy."

"Well said," Richard nodded approvingly. "Precisely why every decision we make must be calculated and cautious. This isn't a simple arbitrage game; it's about anticipating the trajectory of the global economy."

As time passed, John began to grasp Richard's decision-making process. His palms sweated as he processed the data, but he forced himself to focus, meticulously analyzing every detail. He moved beyond the surface numbers, delving into their underlying implications and assessing the potential long-term value of each company. He realized that while short-term volatility carried risks, true investment wisdom lay in finding opportunities amidst the turmoil.

"Remember, John," Richard concluded, "in a crisis, we don't just want to avoid short-term risks, but also look for long-term survival and growth opportunities. The market will eventually recover, but our job is to ensure that our assets not only survive the storm but also emerge stronger."

Richard Harkins was a veteran of Wall Street, active on the front lines of the financial markets since the late 1970s. Despite coming from a middle-class background with no family connections or resources to support his career, he rose through the ranks from an ordinary stockbroker to a senior investment manager at Moorman, driven by his remarkable insight and keen market intuition.

Throughout his career, Richard had witnessed countless market crashes and recoveries, including the 1973 oil crisis, the 1987 Black Monday crash, and the junk bond bubble burst in the late 1980s. These major events exposed him to the market's fragility and unpredictability. They also forged his calm and composed demeanor. He firmly believed that true success in the financial markets came not from luck, but from rationality and decisiveness in the face of turmoil.

Richard had also known personal tragedy. His wife's death in a car accident in the early 1980s had plunged him into a deep depression. But he eventually recovered, and he now imparts the lessons he learned from these experiences to younger colleagues, hoping they will avoid making the same mistakes.

These experiences enabled Richard to maintain remarkable composure in the face of risk and crisis. He often told the young traders, "The market is like life, full of unknown risks. You can't predict what will happen next, but you can be prepared to deal with it." This saying had become a motto within the Moorman Investment Group.

To John, Richard was more than just a successful investor; he was a guiding light in times of trouble. Richard's past experiences had instilled in him a deep empathy for young people. He was willing to spend time mentoring John, seeing in him a burning desire for growth.

John took a deep breath and nodded.

Richard's encouragement brought a wave of warmth, followed by a nagging sense of unease. John realized he couldn't afford to wallow in fear and recalled Richard's words: "Stay calm and learn from your mistakes." This internal struggle spurred him on, reminding him that he had to face the challenges head-on.

"Without Richard's support, I might have already given up," he thought to himself. Richard was not only his mentor but also his pillar of support in the workplace. Although relying on him made John uneasy, it also provided him with a much-needed sense of security.

John felt the invisible pressure of competition, the weight of expectations from those around him. In this high-pressure financial environment, everyone was eager to excel and seize the opportunity to stand out. But as a newcomer, John not only had to strive to integrate into this competitive team but also had to overcome his fear of being overlooked and failing.

"I want to prove myself, but I'm also afraid of failing…" This internal conflict amplified the pressure on John. However, he gradually realized that only by embracing the pressure could he surpass his limitations. This was not just a game of numbers; it was a game of life and career growth.

Post-War Market Stability

On January 17, 1991, a coalition led by the United States launched Operation Desert Storm, conducting a massive airstrike on Iraq, followed by a ground offensive on February 24. Only four days later, the coalition succeeded in driving back Iraqi forces and liberating Kuwait. On February 28, U.S. President George H.W. Bush declared a ceasefire, marking the official end of the war.

With the coalition's victory, tensions in the Middle East began to ease. Oil prices, which had once skyrocketed, plummeted like a punctured balloon, and the market's turbulence subsided. John sat at his desk, his gaze fixed on the ticker display on the trading floor. The wild, heart-stopping fluctuations that once shook him were gradually smoothing out, with market data stabilizing, like the calm after a violent storm at sea, bringing with it a long-awaited sense of peace.

Though the market had stabilized, John's emotions were a complex mix of relief and apprehension. This financial storm had reshaped not just his understanding of the market but also his insight into the forces driving the financial world. He saw now the fragility beneath the market's surface—a delicate balance between panic and trust. The experience had been as much a psychological war as a financial one, revealing his own resilience amid the chaos.

He remembered his initial panic as the market first crashed—each number flashing on the screen like a towering wave, threatening to drag him into a sea of fear and uncertainty. Now, those numbers still danced across the display, but the storm within him had calmed. He felt, for the first time, that he could weather the market's volatility without faltering.

"This is just the beginning," he thought. "A trial by fire, not the end."

Gently, he placed his coffee cup back on the desk, a small but deliberate act that mirrored the market's stability and his own newfound inner calm. He had found his rhythm, a steadiness that no longer wavered with the market's whims.

Around him, the traders resumed their routines. Tom, a seasoned colleague at Moorman with years of experience, walked over with a warm smile.

"John, the market seems to have calmed down a bit. How are you holding up?" Tom asked, nudging him lightly.

John returned the smile, feeling a steady calm within. "I feel much better now. The volatility did shake me up a bit."

"Anyone would be nervous in that situation," Tom reassured him, clapping him on the shoulder. "But you handled it well. You'll get the hang of it."

"I hope so," John replied, but he could sense the growth he had undergone through the crisis.

As Tom walked away, John turned back to his screen, now quiet in its stability. Just as he was about to return to his work, Richard Harkins, his mentor, appeared at his side. Richard's steady gaze and composed demeanor were as reassuring as ever, his eyes reflecting the wisdom of countless storms weathered.

"You did well, John," Richard said, his voice calm and approving. "It's no small feat to remain composed during such market volatility, especially the first time."

John nodded, grateful for Richard's guidance. Through every turn of the crisis, Richard's mentorship had been his anchor. And yet, John sensed this was just the beginning.

Richard's voice dropped slightly, adding a hint of mystery. "The war has just begun."

John looked up at him, a subtle sense of unease tugging at his thoughts, hinting at a greater storm on the horizon. Outside, clouds gathered over the city, darkening the sky as if mirroring the turbulent future that lay ahead. Richard's calm expression concealed a deeper knowledge, a hint that the crisis was far from over.

"This war?" John asked, his voice cautious, anxiety stirring within him.

Richard's subtle smile was unreadable, his eyes reflecting something unspoken. "Yes, the market war. The financial world is never truly calm," he said, his tone low but resonant, each word striking like a warning. "A bigger storm is brewing, and the challenges ahead are far greater than you can imagine. Be prepared, John. The real test is yet to come."

John felt a wave of apprehension but also a growing sense of inner strength. He knew he had chosen a path from which there was no return, a journey that promised even greater trials. Watching Richard walk away, a silent vow took root in his heart—whatever lay ahead, he would face it with unwavering resolve.

Outside, the New York sky remained a serene blue, and the city streets bustled with life. But John knew that beneath this calm exterior, countless storms lay unresolved, waiting. And he was ready to face them all.

THE AGE OF STORMS: JOHN REYNOLDS'
FINANCIAL STRUGGLE

CHAPTER 2

EYE OF THE STORM
1997

The Beginning of the Currency Collapse

Asian countries, particularly Thailand, Indonesia, Malaysia, and South Korea, experienced rapid economic growth in the early 1990s, drawing a massive influx of foreign capital. With money flooding these markets, banks and corporations eagerly borrowed foreign currencies to expand. Yet beneath this veneer of prosperity lay serious vulnerabilities: over-reliance on foreign investment, leveraged borrowing, and inflated asset bubbles.

Thailand, once the icon of the Asian economic miracle, was the first to crack. On July 2, 1997, when the Thai government abandoned its fixed exchange rate policy, the baht crashed, sparking a frantic sell-off by international investors and a wave of panic. The crisis soon swept across Indonesia, Malaysia, and South Korea, the region's economic landscape crumbling like dominoes as currencies and asset prices plummeted.

A trader's cry shattered the morning calm. On the screen, the baht's plummeting exchange rate appeared like a waterfall cascading downward. Suddenly, a young trader shot up from his chair, his face stricken with despair. Clutching his hair, he shouted, "It's over! We're finished!" His voice, thick with fear and helplessness, pierced the tense silence.

Phones rang incessantly, traders' voices rising in urgency and tension. Some scrambled to reassure clients, while others slammed down their phones in frustration and anger. The trading floor buzzed with anxiety, each word and action amplifying the shadow of the crisis.

John stared at the fluctuating numbers on the screen, a sinking feeling growing in his chest as he realized the situation was spiraling out of control. He walked over to Richard's desk, his voice tight with urgency. "Richard, what the hell is going on? The numbers don't add up."

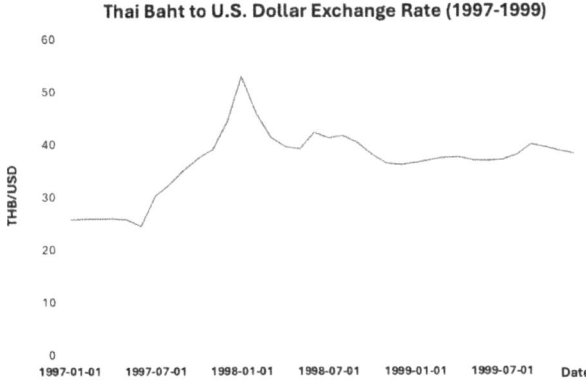

The chart shows the fluctuation of the Thai Baht to U.S. Dollar (THB/USD) exchange rate from 1997 to 1999, with a significant spike in 1998 following the Asian financial crisis. This event had a profound impact on the Thai economy and other Southeast Asian countries, leading to a drastic devaluation of the Thai Baht. Source of data: Federal Reserve Economic Data, FRED.

Richard's brow furrowed as he watched the news on the Bloomberg terminal. "The Thai government has abandoned the fixed exchange rate; the baht is now free-floating." His voice was calm yet serious. "This signals that Thailand's economy has spiraled out of control. International capital is fleeing rapidly."

"How badly will this affect us?" John asked, a sense of foreboding washing over him.

"Very badly," Richard replied, his gaze still locked on the screen. "Our investments in Thailand face significant risks, and this crisis might not stop here. It could spread to other Asian countries, triggering a regional financial storm."

John's heart tightened. This crisis was clearly more complex than the Gulf War and oil crisis, sweeping across the whole of Asia, not just one nation. Richard's words from that time echoed in his mind: "The war may be over, but some things have just begun." Now, those words seemed prophetic.

Moorman Investment Group called an emergency meeting immediately. The atmosphere in the conference room was heavy, almost stifling, as everyone strategized how to deal with the crisis that threatened to engulf all of Asia.

"We should immediately withdraw all investments in Thailand to avoid further losses," Katherine spoke first, her voice decisive. Known for her sharp insights and swift actions, she had earned the respect of her colleagues. She knew that in the face of such a major crisis, acting quickly was essential.

"I agree," Richard nodded. "Our priority now is to preserve capital and avoid risky moves."

"But," Steve countered, "if we withdraw now, we might trigger greater panic and further market turmoil. Besides, I believe the fundamentals of the Asian economies are still sound. This crisis could just be a temporary shock. We should seize this opportunity to buy low, not panic blindly."

"Steve, you're too optimistic," Williams said, his voice edged with warning as he slammed his hand on the table. "This crisis is different. It threatens the entire Asian financial system. We can't take it lightly." He pointed at the world map on the wall, his tone stern. "If this crisis spreads, all of Southeast Asia will be dragged in, and it could impact the global economy." Williams, a seasoned veteran at Moorman, had weathered countless market storms and understood the gravity of the situation.

John listened intently, his mind racing as he absorbed the discussion among these experienced investors. He recalled the financial models he'd studied in college; on paper, all risks seemed quantifiable. But in reality, human nature, politics, and unforeseen events made the market unpredictable.

"We can't be ruled by fear," John reminded himself. He was about to share his thoughts when Williams turned to him and asked, "John, what are your thoughts?"

All eyes turned to John, the weight of expectation pressing on him. His heart pounded as he took a deep breath, steadying himself. "I think… this crisis isn't a coincidence but rather an accumulation of long-standing issues in the Asian economies." His voice grew firmer as he continued, "These countries rely too heavily on foreign investment and exports, neglecting domestic demand and industrial restructuring."

He paused, gathering his thoughts. "Thailand is just the beginning. Other Asian countries face similar vulnerabilities. If they don't take decisive action, this crisis could sweep through Southeast Asia and even ripple across the global economy."

Richard picked up where John left off. "John is right. This crisis reveals the underlying weaknesses of the Asian economies. We need to proceed cautiously."

Williams nodded thoughtfully. "We have to make decisive decisions. This crisis may be more complex than we expect."

Silence fell over the conference room, everyone lost in thought, contemplating the strategies needed to navigate the approaching financial storm.

Capital Flight

"Breaking News on Bloomberg: Asian Financial Crisis Hits Southeast Asia, Several Currencies Plunge." John read the news in disbelief, stunned by the unfolding crisis.

The Wall Street Journal also ran the headline: "Asian Financial Crisis Spreads Like Wildfire in Southeast Asia." Following the collapse of the Thai baht, the Indonesian rupiah, Malaysian ringgit, and

Philippine peso are also experiencing sharp losses, plunging the regional economy into chaos.

Panic gripped the markets. Investors were desperately liquidating assets, leading to a massive outflow of international capital from Asia. Stock markets across the region had crashed, exchange rates continued to fall, and regional financial systems were under unprecedented pressure.

Financial experts warned that the roots of this crisis lay in deep-seated structural weaknesses within Asian economies—such as over-reliance on foreign investment and exports, alongside inadequate financial regulation. Without immediate and decisive intervention, the crisis could escalate further and potentially have global ramifications.

In response, governments across Asia began implementing emergency measures to stabilize their markets. However, despite these efforts, the crisis continued to spread. The future remained highly uncertain, and a swift restoration of confidence in the markets was urgently needed.

John observed the unfolding events in shock. Once-thriving Asian economies were now toppling like dominoes. Stock markets were in free fall, property bubbles had burst, banks were on the verge of collapse, unemployment was skyrocketing, and the streets were filled with protests and despair.

"This is a complete catastrophe," John said to his friend Eric. "I've never witnessed a financial crisis of this magnitude."

Eric, a reporter based in New York, had been covering the Asian financial crisis extensively. He had witnessed firsthand the devastating impact it had on ordinary people, and his heart was heavy with concern and compassion.

"I've been interviewing people affected by the crisis these past few days," Eric said, "and I've seen some truly heartbreaking scenes."

He recounted some of the stories he had gathered during his interviews:

- A small restaurant owner in Thailand was forced to close down after tourist numbers plummeted, leaving him with crippling debt.
- A factory worker in South Korea lost his job due to the factory's closure, and his wife was

also laid off because of soaring prices, plunging their family into hardship.

- A businessman who had invested in Indonesia suffered heavy losses due to the rupiah's crash, and his company was now on the verge of bankruptcy.

"These are just a few examples," Eric continued. "The impact of this crisis is far greater than we can imagine."

"What do you think is the cause of this crisis?" John asked.

"It's a complex issue," Eric replied. "Asian economies have become overly reliant on foreign investment and exports. They have neglected domestic demand and industrial restructuring. Speculative behavior in the international financial markets has also exacerbated the volatility."

"How do you think this crisis will end?" John pressed.

"I'm not sure," Eric admitted. "But I hope that Asian countries can unite and work together to overcome this challenge. I also hope that the international community will offer support so that the Asian economies can recover quickly."

John listened, a knot of worry tightening in his chest. He knew that the fluctuations in the financial markets were not just about numbers; they affected the lives of millions of ordinary people. He thought of Mina's parents, who ran a small grocery store in Seoul, barely making ends meet. Now, with the Korean economy in crisis, their business must be suffering.

John called Mina. "Honey, are you all right?"

"I'm fine," Mina's voice was tinged with fatigue. "The art museum has been packed with visitors lately, and we've been incredibly busy."

"I know," John said, his heart aching for her. "Please take care of yourself."

"And you?" Mina asked with concern. "Is everything okay at work?"

"It's fine. The markets are extremely volatile, so we're all working overtime." John didn't tell Mina about the severity of the crisis; he didn't want to worry her.

"Hmm..." Mina paused, then continued, "By the

way, I spoke to my parents a few days ago. They said business at the store isn't doing well; prices have gone up a lot, and everyone is feeling the pressure. Things aren't looking good in Korea, with many people losing their jobs. Everyone is anxious."

John felt a sharp pang of empathy. He knew he couldn't change the overall economic situation, but he still wanted to do what he could to help those affected.

"I'll send some money to your parents," John offered, trying to make a small contribution in the face of this relentless storm. He knew this financial crisis was not just a market shock but a survival challenge for countless families. He began to reflect on his role as a financial professional, wondering if he could do more than just chase profits and actually help those impacted by the crisis.

This reflection marked a shift in John's understanding of finance.

Under Richard's guidance, John began learning how to identify investment opportunities amidst the crisis. Despite the prevailing panic, he noticed that some companies still had solid fundamentals and future potential. As his learning deepened, John started to propose some initial investment ideas.

"You have a good eye, John," Richard said with a smile. "Times of crisis truly test one's judgment and confidence. We can't let fear dictate our actions. We must remain calm, think rationally, and seize opportunities."

John nodded. He knew this was a valuable learning experience, a test of his abilities, and a challenge from the market. He had to learn to stay calm in this storm, find the glimmer of hope, and turn it into future opportunities.

Confronting the Storm

The shadow of the financial crisis loomed over Wall Street, and every major financial institution was taking action, trying to weather the unexpected storm. Moorman Investment Group was no exception. Emergency meetings were held one after another to discuss strategies. The atmosphere in the conference room was tense; the threat of a market crash hung heavy in the air.

"The situation is dire, gentlemen," Williams said,

his voice steady but his brow furrowed. "We must take decisive measures immediately to protect the company's and our clients' assets."

"I suggest we immediately reduce our exposure in Asian markets, especially Thailand, Indonesia, and Malaysia," Richard added calmly, his eyes reflecting a decision-maker's composure.

"Exactly." Katherine nodded briskly, swiftly picking up a report from the table. "Steve, adjust our asset allocation immediately and reduce our investment ratio in Thailand and Indonesia to the minimum. Tom, you lead the team to review all the funds related to these markets and clear out any projects with excessive risk right away." Her voice was firm and unquestionable as she directed with precision.

She ran her finger across the report, stopping at the data for the United States and Europe. "We should shift our capital to relatively stable markets, such as the U.S. and Europe. Also, companies that rely heavily on exports are at extremely high risk, and we need to be extra cautious," Katherine continued, her tone calm and decisive, her eyes unwavering.

The atmosphere in the conference room shifted

under her direction, everyone tacitly following the instructions of their precise commander. Even in the face of a storm, she maintained her professionalism like a seasoned leader.

John sat in a corner of the conference room, listening to the discussion among these veteran investors. He couldn't help but turn to look at Katherine. Her calmness, decisiveness, and attention to detail filled him with admiration. Seeing her quick response to the crisis, he felt a deeper respect for professionals like Richard and Katherine.

"How can you remain so calm under such pressure?" John finally asked, his voice filled with awe.

Katherine turned to him, her voice calm but firm. "We've all been through many storms, John. Market volatility is the norm, and staying calm and professional is our only way to cope. This is not the time to panic, but to make accurate judgments and take swift action."

Richard paused, then chuckled softly, adding, "Our job is not to avoid storms, but to learn to find opportunities within them. That is the essence of being an investor."

John nodded, feeling a sense of clarity. He finally understood that in the face of such a huge market crisis, these professionals didn't rely on luck but on years of accumulated experience, calm judgment, and decisive action. After the meeting, Richard called John into his office.

"John," Richard's voice was calm but powerful. "I know this crisis has made you uneasy, and that's perfectly normal. Panicking won't help; what we need is to analyze the situation calmly and find concrete measures to minimize losses."

John nodded, though the anxiety in his heart still lingered. "But I still don't know how to deal with such a complex situation." He recalled his experience during the oil crisis. Although he had learned a lot from it, the current crisis seemed even more difficult.

Richard smiled and patted John's shoulder reassuringly. "It is more complex, but that means you'll learn even more." He picked up a document and handed it to John. "Here's a summary of our investment projects in Asia. Take a look."

John opened the file and found that Moorman had a significant investment scale in Thailand, Indonesia, and Malaysia, especially in real estate and infrastructure projects, which were facing extremely high risks. As he looked at the declining figures, his heart sank, the pressure feeling like a mountain weighing on his chest.

"So, how should we respond?" John asked, unable to contain his concern.

"We can consider selling these high-risk assets or hedging to reduce our losses," Richard explained calmly. "For example, we could buy put options on the Thai baht. That way, if the baht continues to depreciate, our losses will be partially offset." He paused, a thoughtful look flashing across his eyes. "At the same time, we should also consider buying some undervalued assets low, hoping for higher returns when the market recovers."

John listened attentively, gradually understanding that risk management wasn't just about cutting losses. It also required a deep understanding of market volatility, investor sentiment, and economic fundamentals. Visions of his younger self, brimming with confidence on his first day, flashed through his mind. Back then, he believed he had mastered all the knowledge and skills necessary to face any challenge the market could throw his way. But now, facing this financial storm, he felt powerless. The gap between theory and reality was far wider than he had ever imagined.

John's thoughts drifted back to the oil crisis a few years ago. At that time, he thought he had seen the worst the market could offer and had managed to survive. But the Asian financial crisis unfolding before him seemed even more unpredictable and complex. Anxiety gnawed at him as he realized that all the formulas and models he'd learned were useless against the real-world crisis unfolding before him.

"This crisis is a valuable learning opportunity for you," Richard said earnestly. "You need to learn to remain calm in the midst of the storm and make rational decisions. That's the most important skill for an investor—managing risk, not just chasing profits."

John nodded seriously, but confusion still lingered in his mind. "Richard, I have a feeling this crisis might affect the entire market, not just our company."

Richard's expression turned grave. He nodded slowly. "You're right. The risks this time are beyond our imagination. Investing is never just a numbers game; it's about people's lives, about the stability of the entire economic system." He paused, a troubled look in his eyes. Gently placing his hand on the table, he said, "You must have a lot of questions. Let's grab a drink tonight and have a good chat."

That evening, a gentle breeze swept through the streets of Wall Street as they walked down a quiet alley toward a secluded bar. It was an old-fashioned establishment, with dim lighting casting a warm glow on the wooden walls and antique decorations, creating a tranquil and calming atmosphere. Richard was dressed in a dark blue suit, the delicate cufflinks glinting faintly in the dim light. John wore a light gray shirt, his tie slightly loosened, revealing a hint of fatigue and unease.

Richard settled into a corner booth by the window. The noise from the bar seemed to fade away, replaced by the soft melody of jazz music drifting through the air. He picked up a glass of whiskey, the amber liquid shimmering gold in the low light, reminiscent of the fluctuating market. He spoke softly, "The market is like the ocean, sometimes calm, sometimes stormy. The key is how you weather the storm."

John pondered for a moment, glancing around the

bar. There weren't many people; a few businessmen in suits conversed in hushed tones, and waiters quietly navigated between tables with trays of drinks. John's gaze returned to Richard, a hint of worry in his eyes. "So, how do we stand firm in such a storm?" he asked.

Richard smiled, taking a sip of his whiskey. His voice held a mentor's wisdom as he replied, "As long as you can analyze calmly and rationally, and take precautions in advance, you can survive in this game. This Asian financial crisis is just one of many storms. There will be more challenges awaiting you in the future."

He placed his glass back on the table, his fingers gently tapping the wooden surface as if contemplating the storms to come. In the dim light, Richard's face seemed particularly profound, like a seasoned sailor who had weathered countless storms yet remained unshaken. His voice was low and firm. "John, this is a learning opportunity, not just about investing, but about how you face every storm in your life."

The neon lights outside flickered through the window, casting dancing shadows on the table. John's confusion and anxiety seemed to ease somewhat in this calm environment. He looked at Richard and nodded, silently resolving to become stronger and calmer in the face of future challenges.

The Spread of the Storm

The severity of the Asian financial crisis far exceeded expectations. Like a raging typhoon, it ripped through Southeast Asia, quickly spreading to other emerging markets. South Korea, Russia, and Brazil were drawn into a vortex of currency devaluation and stock market crashes, with capital fleeing these countries like a flood. Global financial markets plunged into unprecedented panic. Investors scrambled to sell off their assets, desperately seeking refuge in safe havens. The entire market descended into chaos.

Inside Moorman Investment Group, the atmosphere in the trading room was intensely charged. Everyone was busy reacting to the market volatility. The data on the screens danced and swirled, a dizzying spectacle of numbers shifting so rapidly it was almost hypnotic. John sat at his workstation, his heart racing in sync with the market's fluctuations, his palms damp with sweat. He took a deep breath, trying to calm himself, but the anxiety in his chest refused to fade.

"This is truly an unprecedented storm," John muttered, his voice tight with anxiety. He couldn't tear his eyes away from the numbers wildly fluctuating on the screen. "I've never seen anything like it."

Tom, his face pale, could only nod in agreement. "It's beyond what we expected," he whispered, his voice barely audible above the din of the trading floor.

During an emergency meeting, John pointed to the charts and said, "The Korean won has depreciated by over 40%, and the stock market has practically collapsed."

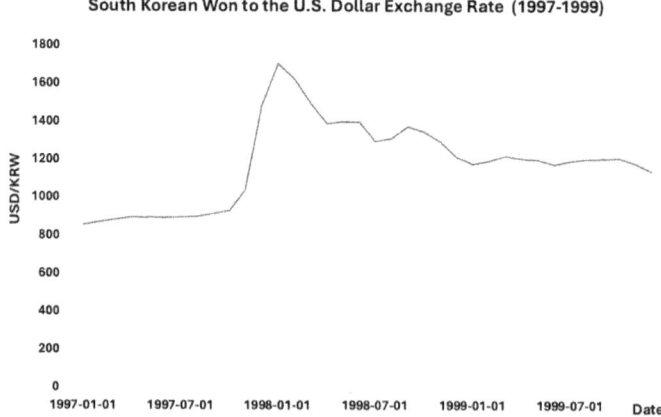

The chart shows the fluctuation of the South Korean Won to U.S. Dollar (KRW/USD) exchange rate from 1997 to 1999, with a significant spike in late 1997 and early 1998 following the Asian financial crisis. This event had a profound impact on the South Korean economy and other East Asian countries, leading to a sharp devaluation of the South Korean Won.
Source of data: Federal Reserve Economic Data, FRED.

"South Korea's debt problem is a ticking time bomb," Richard added, his voice laced with worry.

"Their debt-to-GDP ratio is over 80%. With such a large proportion of short-term foreign debt, any capital flight would leave them unable to service their obligations."

"And that's not all," Catherine continued. "Many of South Korea's large family-run corporations lack transparency and are plagued by nepotism, making them more vulnerable to crises."

William looked around the room, his expression grave. "A collapse in South Korea's economy could spark a global financial crisis, potentially affecting even the U.S. market."

After the meeting, John and his colleagues launched an in-depth analysis of the South Korean economy. They discovered that while the South Korean government had already used a significant portion of its foreign exchange reserves to stabilize the exchange rate, the effects were limited. Non-performing loan ratios in the banking system had soared, and the entire financial system was teetering on the brink of collapse.

"The situation in South Korea is far graver than we anticipated," John wrote in his report. "We must prepare for the worst."

As the crisis spread, Russia also found itself in dire straits. Heavily reliant on energy exports, the decline in international oil prices had dealt a severe blow to the Russian economy. Political instability worsened market uncertainty, as reforms faced heavy resistance and doubts about Russia's future grew.

"I'm worried about a Russian default," John said during a discussion. "This could significantly impact global financial markets, especially institutions with large holdings of Russian bonds."

"You're right," Richard nodded. "Especially Long-Term Capital Management (LTCM)."

"LTCM?" John asked, puzzled.

"LTCM is a hedge fund," Richard explained. "Russia is one of its largest positions. If Russia defaults, LTCM could face bankruptcy."

"Could this trigger a systemic risk?" John asked worriedly.

"Very likely," Richard said gravely. "LTCM's counterparties are spread across the globe. If they collapse, it could trigger a cascade of failures, shaking the stability of the global financial system."

With the situation deteriorating and LTCM teetering on the brink of collapse, Williams, fearing significant losses that could threaten Moorman's survival, called a meeting of the top executives.

"If LTCM goes bankrupt, we need to act immediately to minimize our losses," Williams said in a low voice.

As market pressures mounted, everyone closely watched the fate of LTCM. John continued to analyze the latest data, while discussions within Moorman became increasingly tense.

"LTCM's losses are exceeding our expectations," Catherine said gravely. "Their positions are too large and spread across the globe. They're a ticking time bomb for systemic risk."

Williams turned to John. "The situation is deteriorating. Do you have any additional suggestions?"

Feeling the pressure of this critical moment, John took a deep breath, quickly reviewed the data, and said, "We should further reduce our exposure to high-risk markets, especially Russia and Southeast Asia. At the same time, we should increase our allocation to safe-haven assets, particularly gold and U.S. Treasuries."

After a brief pause, he continued, "Additionally, we can hedge our risk in Russia and Southeast Asia by buying put options. That way, even if the market falls further, we can mitigate our losses through these options."

Richard nodded approvingly. "That's a solid suggestion. We should consider adopting it."

Williams frowned, thinking for a moment, then slowly nodded. "John's suggestion is very reasonable. With the current high market risk, hedging is the best way to effectively control our losses."

"I completely agree," Catherine said firmly. "We must implement this strategy immediately. Time is of the essence."

With LTCM's collapse in 1998, global markets plunged into deeper turmoil. On September 4th, the Dow Jones Industrial Average plummeted 512.61

points, a drop of 4.4%. **The New York Times reported that LTCM's collapse had sparked panic, with investors selling off stocks and bonds, leading to a liquidity crisis.**

Thanks to their prior preparation and decisive response, the Moorman Group successfully avoided the worst-case scenario. John's suggestions and analysis gradually earned the recognition of Richard, Williams, and Catherine. His role became increasingly important, significantly influencing the company's decisions.

This crisis changed John. No longer the inexperienced newcomer, his initial fear had been replaced by rationality and composure. He began to understand that crises always come with opportunities. He learned how to find balance amidst the storm and seize the opportunities that emerged.

Opportunities Amidst the Crisis

On a weekend evening, John and his journalist friend Eric met at a bar in New York, sipping beers and discussing the recent economic crisis.

"This crisis came so suddenly," Eric sighed, taking a sip of his beer. "I've reported on so many companies going bankrupt, seeing people lose their jobs and families falling apart. It's heartbreaking. And here you are, a Wall Street investor, still making money at a time like this?"

John nodded silently, pondering for a moment before replying in a low voice, "Yeah, the market is volatile now, but we're looking for opportunities, especially undervalued companies. But I know many people have lost everything in the process." He looked up slowly, a hint of struggle in his eyes.

Eric's words hit John like a punch to the gut: "In the financial world, there are always winners and losers, and it's always the ordinary people who lose." John took a long sip of his beer, trying to swallow the bitter truth. He knew Eric was right. Every financial crisis, no matter how much manipulation happened on the trading floors of Wall Street, left ordinary people without choices, bearing the brunt. Those who lost their jobs, those who lost their homes—all were victims of this game.

He remembered his youthful idealism, his ambition to change the world. But Wall Street had a way of grinding down such ideals, replacing them with the cold, hard reality of numbers and capital. As an investor, John knew he was part of this system and complicit in its harsh realities. Inner struggles began to surface. He wanted to protect those ordinary people, but he also knew he was powerless to change everything. He had earned a handsome reward, watching his assets double during the crisis, but he couldn't hide the deep-seated guilt within.

He asked himself, "Is this really what I want? Am I really doing the right thing?"

John lowered his head and looked at the beer in his hand. Eric's words echoed in his mind like a refrain: "It's always the ordinary people who lose." The phrase weighed heavily on him. He had thought his success would make the world a better place, but now he had to face the reality that his success came at the expense of others' failures.

"I can't help it, Eric," he finally said, his voice low. "It's a cruel reality. The way Wall Street works doesn't allow for many choices. All I can do is try to protect the company and my clients' assets and find a way to survive this storm."

But even as he said these words, he felt another voice within him resisting. He knew he didn't want to completely succumb to this system, yet he was aware this struggle wouldn't end easily. The opportunities and money brought by the financial crisis grew, pulling him deeper into the system's grip. The ruthlessness and cruelty of Wall Street were not what he sought, but he had gone too far to easily turn back.

The silence between them deepened, and the noise of the bar seemed to fade away. John felt trapped in a dilemma he couldn't escape. He longed to break free from the status quo, but he was also unable to shake off the chains of reality. He began to realize that this financial storm was not just a battle for survival but also an internal war.

During a discussion about an internet investment project, Catherine specifically asked John to share his insights. She pointed out that as the Asian market gradually stabilized, many local tech companies were beginning to recover, especially those that had shown resilience during the crisis and were attracting global investors.

"John, some of the companies involved in this project are Asian tech companies that have been less affected by the financial crisis. What do you think of the risks and potential of these companies?" she asked, anticipation in her voice.

John thought carefully before responding, "Although the financial crisis has had a significant impact, it has also created many opportunities in the market, especially in the internet sector—demand still exists despite volatility. With careful risk management, these companies have the potential to generate long-term returns."

Williams nodded in agreement, saying, "John's analysis is very accurate. The potential of the Asian market cannot be ignored, and we should seize this opportunity."

This discussion highlighted John's growing influence. He was no longer just a bystander in meetings but actively participated in decision-making and investment discussions. When the Moorman team considered acquiring a newly emerging internet company, NeuraTech, John had the first opportunity to offer his perspective. Although NeuraTech's stock price had soared due to market overheating, its core technology and long-term potential were still worth noting.

As John and the Moorman team delved deeper into discussions about acquiring NeuraTech, he suddenly received a call from Jim, a friend at Barclays Bank and his competitor.

"John, I heard that your Moorman Group is eyeing NeuraTech," Jim said with a hint of provocation. "To be honest, we're also considering acquiring this company. It seems we're competitors again."

"Another round of competition?" John smiled, but he knew in his heart that this competition would not be easy. Barclays' acquisition strategy was clearly focused on quickly merging with promising tech companies. They were particularly interested in NeuraTech's technology in cybersecurity and data processing, which were core areas in the Internet age.

The Moorman team faced multiple pressures from both the market and within. There was internal strife as well; the investment department was eager to ride the wave of the internet revolution, pushing for the acquisition, while the risk management department worried about NeuraTech's high valuation, fearing that it was a bubble that could eventually lead to huge losses for the company.

During in-depth discussions on the NeuraTech acquisition, John recognized the company's technology as crucial for the future development of the internet. Although its current market valuation was high, NeuraTech's core technology had a deep competitive advantage in cybersecurity and data processing. John knew that even if the bubble burst, such a technology company could still hold long-term value.

This competition was more than just a battle between Moorman and Barclays for control of NeuraTech; it was a test of their understanding of the evolving internet landscape. John had to find a balance between internal contradictions and external competition and develop a strategy that could both protect the company from the bursting of bubbles and seize the opportunities of the internet revolution.

"John, do you really think it's right for us to acquire NeuraTech?" Tom asked, looking at him with doubt. "Are we taking advantage of the situation?"

John was silent. He understood Tom's concerns but also knew that if they missed this opportunity, NeuraTech might be acquired by other competitors, which would be a loss for the company's technology and employees.

"I understand your concerns, Tom," John said sincerely. "But we can also see this acquisition as an investment—an investment in the future of Korea. If we can help NeuraTech recover, it will benefit not only the company but also Korea's economy."

A few days later, Williams instructed John and Richard to fly to Seoul to negotiate with NeuraTech's management. When their plane landed at Incheon International Airport, the cold air of Seoul hit John's face as he stepped out of the cabin. He saw pedestrians on the street walking in a hurry, with anxious expressions on their faces. The impact of the financial crisis was everywhere, but he also sensed a resilient spirit in the city that had not been defeated by the crisis.

With an understanding nod and a smile, John began speaking in fluent Korean. "I understand your concerns, especially at this moment. NeuraTech represents more than just a company; it's a symbol of Korea's technological prowess. We have no intention of interfering with your autonomy. Instead, we want to support you during this challenging time and help NeuraTech better address these challenges."

As John expressed his opinion in Korean, the NeuraTech management team was visibly impressed by his language skills. As a foreign investor, John had clearly put in extra effort to understand their culture, which put them slightly at ease. This was one of his carefully prepared strategies. He knew that in Korean culture, respect and understanding of local values were crucial, especially for a long-established company like NeuraTech.

Next, John further broke the deadlock by demonstrating his cultural sensitivity. "NeuraTech is the pride of Korea, and we at Moorman fully respect that. Our goal is not control but cooperation. We can keep NeuraTech's leadership and core technical team intact, ensuring that your culture and vision continue."

The CEO listened intently, his stern expression softening slightly as his eyebrows unfurrowed. His doubts about foreign investment were not solely about funding but about concerns over control of the company. He worried that Moorman would forcefully change NeuraTech's core culture and treat it merely as an asset.

Perceiving this, John elaborated further, "Moorman wants to support your vision, not replace it.

In fact, we believe in the unlimited potential of NeuraTech. We are willing to invest more capital specifically for research and development, which will not only help the company overcome the current crisis but also ensure that you continue to maintain a leading position in the global technology market."

With that, he placed a detailed report on the table, outlining Moorman's investment plan with a strong emphasis on technological innovation and team stability. John had carefully selected the key points, focusing on the long-term development and technological autonomy that Korean companies cared most about, which made the CEO and other management team members start to seriously consider his proposal.

The CFO of NeuraTech flipped through the report, frowning as he asked, "The amount of investment you proposed is very attractive, but we are still concerned about whether you will eventually interfere with our operational decisions. Although Moorman has a good reputation globally, we need to ensure that NeuraTech can continue to move forward in its own way."

John smiled and responded, "That's exactly our commitment. We won't interfere with your day-to-day operations. What we provide is resources and support to help NeuraTech overcome this crisis and remain competitive in the future technology market. Moorman's commitment to you is not just financial support but also includes global market development and strategic cooperation."

He cleverly used some cultural terms in Korean, such as **"hamkke himeul mo-euda"** (working together to achieve a common goal), to strengthen the sense of cooperation. This subtle cultural touch made the management team feel that he truly respected and understood Korean culture.

Finally, John proposed a new cooperative condition: Moorman would establish a dedicated innovation fund, allowing NeuraTech to freely use this fund for research and development over the next five years without Moorman's approval. In this way, NeuraTech could guarantee its technological autonomy while also receiving financial support.

The CEO exchanged a few words with the CFO and then nodded slowly. "We will carefully consider this proposal. Your sincerity has shown us the possibility of cooperation."

John felt a sense of relief. He knew the negotiation was far from over, but he had found a breakthrough. For this proud Korean tech company, respecting their culture and autonomy was more important than any number. He knew deep down that this acquisition was not just a business negotiation but also a cross-cultural intellectual game.

As John and Richard walked out of NeuraTech's headquarters, feeling a sense of accomplishment, John's phone suddenly rang. It was a call from the Moorman New York office.

"John, there's urgent news," Tom said urgently on the other end of the line. "Barclays Bank is moving quickly. They've just made a more attractive acquisition offer to NeuraTech, and their terms are more favorable than ours."

John's heart sank. Victory, it seemed, was far from assured. Although he and Richard had just finished the negotiation, Barclays' move was clearly intended to disrupt things at the last minute.

"Damn it, Barclays is always like this," Richard muttered, frowning. "They're playing a game of ultimatum."

"We have to respond immediately; we can't let Barclays take control," John said, forcing himself to stay calm. He quickly reviewed the negotiation process and pondered how to strengthen Moorman's terms to prevent NeuraTech from being poached by Barclays.

With time running out, John decided to reconnect with NeuraTech's management right away. They returned to the building, and this time the atmosphere was even more tense, as they knew this negotiation had entered its most critical stage. John stated Moorman's advantages more directly, emphasizing Moorman's global market influence and resources. Additionally, he proposed a new condition, promising that Moorman would increase its investment in NeuraTech's technology research and development to ensure its competitiveness in the market.

"I know Barclays can offer a lot," John looked directly into the CEO's eyes, his tone firm. "But what Moorman can give you is not just funds, but a long-term partnership. We have the ability to help you go further, not only to overcome the current crisis but also to steadily develop in the global market."

A tense silence fell over the meeting room, the pressure mounting with Barclays' unexpected proposal.

Just as John felt the situation slipping away, the CFO whispered something to the CEO, who then sighed and slowly said, "We've considered it, and Moorman's long-term support is more important to us."

At that moment, a stone in John's heart finally fell. Moorman had successfully defeated Barclays and won the acquisition battle. As John and Richard walked out of NeuraTech's building, they exchanged satisfied glances. Although the struggle was more difficult than they had expected, they had succeeded in the end. Barclays' counterattack, though fierce, had proven ineffective against Moorman's strategic approach.

"Well done, John!" Richard patted him on the shoulder excitedly. "You did a great job in this acquisition. Your Korean language and data analysis skills are impeccable."

"Thank you, Richard," John replied modestly. "I still have a lot to learn."

Richard chuckled. "Your performance has exceeded my expectations, John. But don't forget, the market is always full of variables, and this is just your first step. There will be more challenges ahead, and you need to learn to stay calm under even greater pressure."

Just as John and Richard were preparing to return to New York, John's phone rang. It was a call from the Moorman New York office.

"John, we've noticed unusual fluctuations in the stocks of some U.S. internet companies, especially large technology companies, and their stock prices are rising sharply."

As John stood on the streets of Seoul, the cool breeze brushing against his face seemed to sober him up. But beneath the surface, a dark ambition was stirring within him. He looked at the bustling city, with its rushing crowds and flashing neon lights—a world of limitless opportunity. The skyscrapers on both sides of the street rose like symbols of power, as if hinting that those who controlled capital could climb infinitely—and perhaps he could, too.

A voice deep inside him became clear: "Isn't this what you've always wanted? Success, power, influence—they're all within your reach."

John recalled his early days on Wall Street, filled with ideals and the hope of changing the world through finance. But as his position in Moorman solidified, that pure idealism had been eroded by the fierce competition and desire surrounding him. In the past, he might have felt sympathy for those who had lost everything in the crisis, but now he found himself growing accustomed to this ruthless world and even beginning to relish the game.

"You've changed," whispered another voice within him. "Where is the you who once sought fairness and justice?"

He looked toward Namsan Tower in the distance, a symbol of resilience and the city's indomitable spirit. Yet he sensed that this resilience wasn't only about survival but also about achieving power and control. The feeling was intoxicating, as if the whole city were urging him to pursue more money and status.

"Is this really what I want?" The struggle in his heart grew more apparent. "Or is it just consuming me?"

The Korean conversations and the sound of traffic around him pulled him back to reality. He felt as though he were standing at the threshold of power, and one more step would open the world to him completely. But he also understood that crossing this threshold would change everything—not only his career but also his values and his soul.

"Perhaps this is the truth of Wall Street," he murmured to himself. "Here, only the strong survive, and all you can do is become strong and take control."

He took a slow, steady breath, feeling the desire coursing through his body. Those voices that had once questioned his path, that had made him feel moral confusion, were gradually fading. Replacing them was a sense of power, an intoxicating drive that made his heart race and brought a hint of excitement.

"Maybe I deserve this," he said softly, his eyes growing resolute. "No more hesitation, no more struggle—this is the path I'm going to take."

Standing on the bustling streets of Seoul, John no longer felt like the idealistic young man he had once been. Now, he was a man who had weathered the storms of Wall Street and could thrive in this unforgiving world. He accepted the reality that if he didn't actively pursue power, it would slip away, and he would never have the chance to turn back.

At that moment, he felt he had completely transformed. He was no longer just surviving; he was seeking dominance. He was no longer a bystander concerned with morality but a player plunging headfirst into the abyss of ambition. That desire, like a flood, overwhelmed him.

THE AGE OF STORMS: JOHN REYNOLDS'
FINANCIAL STRUGGLE

CHAPTER 3

THE MOMENT OF DISILLUSIONMENT 2000

The Madness of Tech Stocks

In early 2000, as internet technology rapidly evolved, global fascination with the digital future sent tech stocks soaring. Corporations of all sizes were rushing to establish an online presence, fueling investors' sky-high expectations for these burgeoning companies. Stock prices escalated at an unprecedented rate, and the market was permeated with manic optimism. Company valuations reached dizzying heights, with media outlets flooded with hyperbolic predictions and glowing forecasts. This "internet revolution" was seen as an unstoppable force—a tsunami of innovation attracting global capital with an almost religious fervor. The Nasdaq index climbed higher and higher, setting new records almost daily.

Sensational headlines screamed from newspapers and websites, whipping the public into a frenzy:

"The Internet Will Change the World! Invest in These 10 Companies and Retire a Millionaire!"

"Tech Stocks Soaring! Is Your Wallet Ready? Missing Out on This Opportunity Will Be Your Biggest Regret!"

"E-commerce Will Replace Traditional Retail! Invest Now to Secure Your Future!"

Time magazine proclaimed on its cover: "The Internet: The New Gold Rush!" while **the Wall Street Journal headlined: "Tech Stocks Lead the Market, Economic Boom Just Around the Corner!"** On television, charismatic anchors excitedly predicted, **"This is an unprecedented technological revolution. Seize this wave, and you'll be the next billionaire!"**

The investment frenzy permeated every aspect of society. Online stock discussion forums popped up like mushrooms after the rain, with investors passionately debating tech stocks and sharing insider tips. The usage of online trading platforms surged as even housewives and students joined the investment frenzy. Owning tech stocks had become more than a financial investment; it was a status symbol. In offices, discussions about stocks dominated conversations, and everyone eagerly shared their investment insights. It seemed that the more tech stocks you owned, the more successful you were.

John sat in his office at Moorman Investment Group, surrounded by the laughter and excited chatter of his colleagues, all celebrating their investment victories. Watching the wild fluctuations of tech stock prices on his screen, a sense of unease crept into his heart. Despite the market's exuberance, he knew such irrational exuberance was often followed by a painful crash. On the streets, people buzzed about tech stocks. Over lunch, he overheard strangers excitedly discussing a newly listed internet company, brimming with optimism. At an investment seminar, a speaker passionately painted a picture of the limitless potential of the internet, with the audience nodding in agreement, their eyes gleaming with the promise of wealth.

At a company meeting, Williams, radiating an almost messianic zeal, declared, "Tech stocks will lead us into a new era. This is our greatest investment opportunity!" He waved his arms enthusiastically and proclaimed, "The internet will change everything!" John sat in a corner of the meeting room, listening to these ambitious statements but couldn't fully immerse himself in the optimism. He remembered the Asian financial crisis a few years ago, when a similar frenzy had ended in disaster for many investors. He knew that the current boom would eventually burst, like any other economic bubble. But these sober thoughts seemed so out of place in the current atmosphere.

Although he was deeply concerned about the market's irrational exuberance, John couldn't deny the allure of the enormous wealth that the "Internet revolution" promised. The rapid rise in stock prices, the extreme optimism of the market, and the sense that every decision could yield a huge payoff were thrilling. This feeling of investment success was a powerful force, driving him to chase even greater returns.

"John, this is our chance to get in," his colleague Steve said eagerly, leaning closer and lowering his voice conspiratorially. "Have you seen those companies? Their stock prices are skyrocketing! If we don't seize this opportunity, we'll miss out on an entire era!" He paused, his eyes gleaming with excitement. "Like eToys," Steve continued, opening his screen. "Its stock price has tripled in just a few months. Who would have thought? This is the kind of opportunity we need to grab!"

John forced a smile and said nothing. He knew there was some truth to what Steve was saying, but deep down, a nagging sense of unease persisted. On the surface, he agreed with Steve, but inside, he wondered, how long can this madness last? Is there a crisis lurking beneath this euphoria?

As time went on, John felt increasing pressure within the company. Management constantly urged them to increase their investments in tech stocks, emphasizing that this was a crucial moment for the group's expansion. In meetings, senior executives repeated the same mantra: not participating in this tech revolution would mean missing out on a once-in-a-lifetime opportunity, even risking Moorman Group's survival. Surrounded by such unwavering optimism, John began to waver. Although he knew the tech stock bubble was risky, the constant pressure and discussions with colleagues gradually clouded his judgment. He began to question himself: Am I being overly cautious? Is this truly a revolutionary change? Am I missing out on something big?

Eventually, John decided to increase his investment in tech stocks. He joined his colleagues in enthusiastically discussing the skyrocketing companies. At company investment meetings, he even started making optimistic comments about tech stocks, trying to fit in with the group. However, no matter how much he tried to embrace the hype, a deep-seated unease remained.

Every night, as he lay in bed, John wondered if this

tech frenzy could truly last. He knew that market booms were often followed by busts, but the current atmosphere made him feel isolated. He could almost hear it: the faint sound of a bubble bursting. A faint alarm bell, nearly drowned out by the noise of the market and the cheers of victory, echoed persistently in the depths of his mind.

One night, this pressure even seeped into his dreams. He dreamed he was standing on a towering skyscraper, the wind whipping through his hair, surrounded by people cheering and pointing excitedly at the glittering cityscape below. They laughed and seemed to have the world at their fingertips. But John felt an indescribable fear, as if he were standing on the edge of a cliff. The building began to sway slightly, and he could feel the floor beneath his feet trembling, as if it could collapse at any moment. Yet, the people around him remained oblivious, lost in their euphoria.

He tried to escape the building, but his feet seemed rooted to the spot. He tried to shout a warning to the people around him, but his voice was swallowed by the wind. Fear overwhelmed him as the building shook more violently, and with a loud crash, the floor gave way, and the cheers turned into screams.

John woke up gasping for breath, his heart pounding. He sat up in bed, staring out at the night sky, and the fear from his dream lingered. Even though the dream was over, the shadow in his heart remained.

And so, John entered the tech stock frenzy with mixed emotions, knowing that this bubble was waiting to burst.

Signs of the Bubble

In the spring of 2000, the tech stock boom began to show signs of trouble. High-flying internet companies like Pets.com and Boo.com, once darlings of the market, filed for bankruptcy one after another. These companies, fueled by hype and speculation, had attracted significant investments, but their flawed business models ultimately led to their collapse after exhausting investors' funds, signaling the impending burst of the dot-com bubble.

News reports were filled with stories of these bankruptcies, focusing particularly on Pets.com. "This online pet supply retailer was known for its adorable sock puppet mascot and extravagant advertising," one report noted. "However, it ultimately failed to establish a sustainable profit model in the face of fierce competition, resulting in its bankruptcy in November 2000." Another report dissected Boo.com's downfall: "This Swedish online fashion retailer, once popular for its personalized clothing designs and express delivery service, declared bankruptcy in May 2000 due to overexpansion and a broken capital chain."

These reports filled John with a deep sense of unease. He recalled historical economic bubbles: the tulip mania of the 17th century and the South Sea Bubble of the 18th century—all instances of rampant speculation that ultimately ended in collapse, leaving investors with devastating losses. Despite the seemingly unstoppable rise of tech stocks, John knew that lurking behind this prosperity was the shadow of a crisis.

During his university years, John delved into the theory of economic bubbles in a class taught by renowned economics professor Peter Sutherland. Professor Sutherland emphasized the phenomenon of "rational irrationality," where market participants, despite knowing prices were inflated, would still follow the herd, hoping to profit from the frenzy. This solidified John's belief that the current tech stock surge was a bubble waiting to burst. He also recalled Professor Sutherland's discussions of the "efficient market hypothesis" and "modern portfolio theory." Although these theories emphasize that market prices reflect all available information, John knew that when speculation runs rampant, these principles often fail, increasing the risk of a crash.

Determined to mitigate the risk, John decided to warn the company's senior management by writing a detailed report. He analyzed the potential risks in the current tech stock market and cited Professor Sutherland's frequent warning: "Excessive market optimism is often a precursor to a crisis." He remembered the professor's words: "When everyone in the market believes that prices will only go up, that's when the risk is greatest." In his report, he recommended that the company reduce its tech stock holdings and adopt a hedging strategy. However, his report was largely ignored. Moorman Group's executives believed the tech stock rally was still strong, focusing instead on seizing opportunities rather than considering an exit.

In a meeting, Williams stood before the projection screen, addressing the company's core team, his voice filled with excitement. "We have breaking news today. The Federal Reserve just announced a 25-basis-point cut to the federal funds rate. This is the fifth rate cut this year! The market has reacted very strongly, with technology stocks leading the rally and the Dow Jones Industrial Average surging!" He paused, his gaze sweeping across the room as a confident smile appeared on his face. "This technological revolution is far from over, everyone. This is our opportunity!"

Williams continued, "We, Moorman Investment Group, must seize this golden opportunity! Now is the perfect time for expansion. According to our latest research, the technology sector has a growth potential of over 30% within the next five years. We plan to complete three major acquisitions this year to expand our presence in the technology sector and increase our investment in emerging markets." He emphasized his words, as if declaring an unshakeable future. "We will expand the company's assets and are confident we can double our profits within the next two years!"

"The growth curves and market analysis reports flashing on the big screen fueled their belief in the immense potential of this 'technological revolution' and the abundant returns it promised."

"Williams drove his point home. "This isn't just a temporary trend; it's a global transformation. Moorman Investment Group has a real chance to lead this revolution."

Applause and nods echoed Williams's words, filling the meeting room with an air of excitement. During the discussions that followed, Richard turned to John, a hint of disdain in his voice. "John, you're too conservative. Tech stocks are the future; we're witnessing a historical transformation! If we pull out now, we'll not only miss this golden opportunity but also risk being left behind by the market."

John tried to explain his concerns, voicing his worries about market risks and the cautionary tales of past bubbles, but Richard was clearly uninterested. "We need to embrace this revolution," Richard stated firmly. "Now is the time to double down, not back down!"

As time went on, the company's internal atmosphere grew increasingly feverish. Almost everyone was convinced that tech stocks would continue to soar, with no reason to doubt that this upward trend would ever stop. John's warnings were completely ignored. His concerns about market risks seemed out of place in this exuberant atmosphere. Senior management even began to see him as overly cautious and unable to keep up with the times.

Whenever he tried to raise risk warnings in meetings, his colleagues responded with dismissive replies, their eyes filled with disapproval, as if he had become an anomaly in this era of frenzied investment.

"John, if you back out now, you're giving up the best opportunity of your life," Steve told him after a meeting. "Look at those tech companies—their stock prices are hitting new highs almost every week. If we don't seize this opportunity, we're essentially giving up our ticket to financial freedom!"

Steve's words sowed seeds of doubt in John's mind. The market frenzy and his colleagues' influence made him question his judgment. Perhaps Richard and Steve were right? Maybe this was indeed a revolution that would change the future. Such an opportunity, once missed, might never come again.

Late that night, alone in the office, John sat facing the fluctuating graphs of tech stock prices, his internal struggle raging within him. His fingers trembled slightly on the keyboard, a cold sweat beading on his forehead. He knew he was standing at a crucial crossroads, with a safe retreat on one side and the allure of infinite wealth on the other. John's heartbeat quickened, the deep-seated unease within him casting a persistent shadow.

"Is this really worth it?" The voice of doubt echoed in his mind. Visions of bankrupt companies, of investors once celebrated now ruined, flashed through his mind. He pictured families devastated, their dreams shattered by the bursting bubble. But as he looked again at the ever-climbing curve on the screen, his reason seemed to drown in his yearning for success. "Maybe this time is different. This is the Internet age—a revolution," he forced himself to believe.

Despite knowing the immense risk, the battle between reason and emotion raged within him. In the end, emotion triumphed. He opened his personal investment account and started entering numbers, his fingers lingering on each key longer than usual, as if waiting for a miracle to stop him. But finally, he took a deep breath and pressed the "Confirm" button.

The next day, John met his longtime friend and loan manager, Jerry, at a coffee shop near Wall Street. They sat by the window, overlooking the bustling street.

The noise and movement, the honking cars, all seemed insignificant compared to the future wealth they were discussing.

Jerry looked at John, his brow furrowed with concern. "John, are you sure you want to do this?" His voice was filled with genuine worry, his fingers tapping the rim of his coffee cup. "This isn't just about using your house as collateral; you're also taking out a large personal loan. What if the market crashes? You won't just lose money; you'll lose your house."

John lowered his gaze to the table, the internal struggle resurfacing. Jerry's words pierced the fear deep within him. "I know the risks are high," he said, forcing a smile. "But this is a chance to change my future. The internet is developing so rapidly—everyone's saying it's a revolution. If I miss this, I might never get another opportunity like it."

Jerry sighed, leaning back in his chair, his eyes filled with doubt. "But what about your family? You have children to support. If this investment fails, how will you face them?" Jerry's tone grew heavier, as if hoping this last question would make John reconsider.

John took a deep breath, gripping his coffee cup as

if it were his last lifeline. He glanced out the window, envisioning a future where everything went smoothly, where he would have enough capital to become a market winner, free from financial worries. "I won't let it crash," he finally said, a hint of determination in his voice, as if trying to convince himself. "I will succeed this time."

Jerry was silent for a moment, then sighed. "Alright, since you've made up your mind, I'll help you with the loan. But promise me, don't take any more risks."

They shook hands and said goodbye. As Jerry left, John remained seated, his friend's words echoing in his mind. He knew there was no turning back. All his hopes were pinned on this tech stock investment. If he succeeded, he would reach the pinnacle of his career; if he failed, the consequences would be devastating.

Back at the office, the streets outside were quiet, the day's bustle long gone. In the stillness of the night, only the cold light of the computer screen illuminated John's face. The office was so silent that the only sound was the hum of the air conditioning. This silence amplified the invisible pressure weighing on him. He sat at his desk, unconsciously tapping his fingers on the surface, with the scattered documents and the fluctuating tech stock prices on the screen fueling his anxiety.

He glanced at the clock on the wall, the ticking hands marking the passage of time, yet the struggle in his heart remained. His fingers trembled slightly on the keyboard, each keystroke a gamble on his future. The empty office, like his heart, was filled with a suffocating silence.

The office's tranquility was a stark contrast to the turmoil within him. On the surface, everything seemed calm, like the seemingly prosperous stock market. But John knew that this tranquility concealed the ever-present risk of a sudden eruption, like an unstable bubble ready to burst, shattering everything in its wake.

The Bubble Burst

March 10th, 2000. The day the tech stock frenzy came to a screeching halt. The Nasdaq Composite Index surged to an unprecedented high of 5,132 points, only to plummet sharply almost immediately. As the opening bell sounded, traders on the floor roared, the index breaking past 5,100, champagne corks popping in premature celebration. Hugs, cheers, and laughter filled the room, but jubilation was fleeting. Within half an hour, the index reversed, plunging at a breathtaking pace. Laughter quickly turned to stunned silence. Faces once flushed with excitement now froze in disbelief.

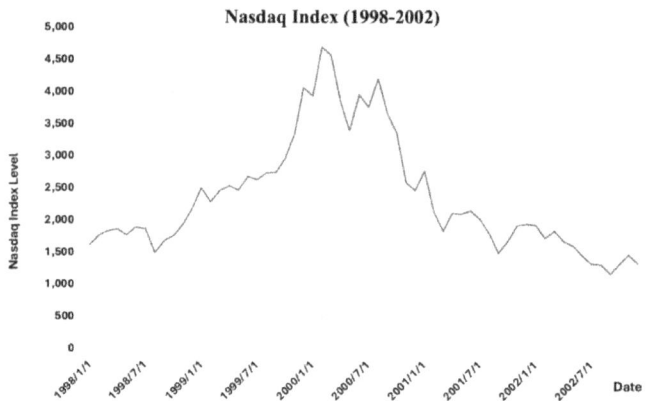

The chart shows the Nasdaq Index from 1998 to 2002, peaking in early 2000 during the dot-com bubble. After the bubble burst, the index dropped sharply, reflecting the collapse of many internet companies and the subsequent market downturn.
Source of Data: Federal Reserve Economic Data (FRED).

John watched stock prices freefall on the screen, feeling as if he were strapped to a runaway rollercoaster hurtling into darkness. Panic seized him, his heart pounding and cold sweat prickling his forehead. He wanted to turn away, to shut out the sight of those red numbers multiplying before him, but he couldn't tear his eyes away, transfixed by the spectacle of the crash. With each drop, a knot tightened in his stomach, fear spreading through his body like a shockwave.

At first, he clung to hope, assuring himself it was just a correction. "Maybe the market will bounce back," he muttered under his breath. But with every passing minute, the decline only accelerated, swallowing that hope whole. Breaths came in shallow gasps as the crushing realization hit him: he had made a monumental error, one that would change everything.

Self-reproach soon consumed him. John's mind flooded with regrets, an endless loop of "what ifs" and "if onlys." If only he'd heeded his warnings, if only he hadn't joined the frenzy, if only he had resisted the pressure from colleagues. Each regret twisted deeper into his gut.

As his losses mounted, fear became all-consuming. He began calculating, tallying up what he'd lose, the devastation it would wreak on his family. All his dreams—the home he'd bought, his children's education, the security he'd envisioned for his retirement—felt like shards of broken glass scattered across the floor. Helplessness weighed down on him, his world shattering as he stood by, powerless to stop it.

His phone buzzed. Mina's name appeared on the screen, and he reluctantly answered, forcing steadiness into his voice.

"John, how's it going today?" she asked, sounding cheerful. "I just wanted to remind you—don't forget about Alex's school recital tonight."

For a second, John was silent, struggling to hide the despair clawing at him. "Yeah, of course," he replied, his voice strained. "I'll be there."

"Are you okay?" she pressed, detecting something off in his tone.

"Just… a tough day," he murmured. "I'll explain later."

"Alright," Mina said softly. "Just remember, whatever it is, we're in this together."

Her words hit him hard, mingling love with the weight of his hidden shame. He knew he couldn't bring himself to confess the full extent of the losses yet. Alone in the trading room, John felt as if he were falling into an endless abyss, trapped in the consequences of his choices.

The market closed, but the nightmare continued.

John was buried in debt, his savings wiped out. The bank foreclosed on his house, forcing him and Mina to move into a cramped rental. The financial strain was crushing. In the quiet hours of the night, he would replay the plummeting charts in his mind, those glaring red numbers seared into his memory. He loathed his own greed and recklessness, despising himself even more for dragging his family into this disaster.

Over the following months, John's spirit collapsed. He questioned every decision he had ever made, doubting his worth. Mina's parents, who relied on him after closing their small grocery store in the crisis, weighed heavily on his conscience. With each pang of guilt, John's self-blame intensified.

His pursuit of short-term gains now seemed reckless; his disregard for risk was unforgivable. Only now did he truly grasp the folly of putting all his eggs in one basket, especially in a market so volatile.

As the bubble burst, news reports were filled with stories of failing companies. The bankruptcy of eToys became a symbol of this catastrophe. The online toy retailer's servers crashed under the weight of holiday traffic, leading to its collapse. Thousands of employees were left jobless. WorldCom, after its accounting fraud was exposed, quickly went bankrupt, resulting in tens of thousands of layoffs.

John's friends, the Smiths, saw their entire savings wiped out. They had planned to use their tech stock investments to fund their children's college education, but their dreams were shattered. Their children's aspirations had to be abandoned, and the parents returned to the workforce. Mina's friend, Mr. Lee, suffered a similar fate; he lost his entire retirement fund in tech stocks and was forced back into the job market.

Yet, the most painful consequence involved John's close friend, David. On John's advice, David had invested his savings in tech stocks. With the bubble's collapse, David's investment evaporated, leaving him in financial ruin. Resentment toward John consumed him, and he even threatened legal action, which intensified John's guilt. John wanted to reach out, to explain that he never anticipated this collapse, but each time he tried, words failed him. He was left paralyzed by helplessness and remorse.

That day, David stormed into John's office, his footsteps like a thunderous drum. His face was livid, his jaw clenched tightly, and his eyes were ablaze with rage. Before John could react, David slammed his hands on the desk, scattering papers and nearly knocking over John's water cup.

"This is the advice you gave me?" David's voice, sharp and cutting, tore through the silence, striking John's heart. "You ruined me! You ruined everything!" Each word was a blade, piercing through John's nerves.

John struggled to meet David's eyes, his mind spinning. How could everything have gone so wrong? He wanted to explain, to offer some words of comfort, but nothing he could say would justify the devastation.

David's nostrils flared as he leaned in closer, pointing a trembling finger. "You told me this was an opportunity, that this was my chance to change my future—and what happened? Everything's destroyed!" His voice, hoarse with despair, trembled with the force of his emotions.

John sank back in his chair, his hands clenching involuntarily, knuckles white. His chest felt like a boulder was pressing down, making it hard to breathe. "I... I didn't expect this to happen..." he stammered, his voice barely audible, knowing how hollow it sounded.

David cut him off, roaring, "No! You didn't know

what you were doing! You pushed me into the abyss, and now I have nothing!"

Silence filled the room after David's words faded, but John could still feel the weight of his friend's rage pressing down on him. He looked away, guilt gnawing at him, each passing second dragging him deeper into the chasm of regret.

With the bursting of the dot-com bubble, John felt the ruthless force of the financial market like never before. Every day, he was suffocated by the plummeting numbers, his once-steady confidence replaced by waves of fear and regret. The losses haunted him like a recurring nightmare, a heavy weight pressing down on his chest day and night. He felt as though he were standing on the edge of a cliff, with the ground crumbling beneath him, each crash pushing him closer to the brink.

The financial losses were painful enough, but the relentless self-blame was unbearable. He replayed every decision, every misstep, each choice that had led him and those around him into ruin. He isolated himself, distancing himself from friends and family, consumed by loneliness and sinking into a deep depression.

But even in the depths of despair, John began to reflect on his past. He recalled those short-term gains that once made his heart race, which had now turned into one trap after another. He gradually realized that not every risk could lead to success, and his relentless pursuit of short-term returns was precisely what had driven him into this crisis. Each loss and mistake became an opportunity to reassess his investment strategies. Though this painful experience was destructive, it marked the beginning of a new journey for him.

The Personal Investor's Disaster

On a sweltering night, John and Mina sat in their cramped rented apartment, the silence heavy with unspoken anxiety and simmering tension. The sparse furnishings and dim lighting were a constant reminder of all they had lost. The air felt thick with a suffocating pressure, threatening to break at any moment.

"What are we going to do now?" Mina finally broke the stifling silence, her voice strained with exhaustion and barely concealed fury. Her voice rose sharply, tears glistening in her eyes. "The money's gone, the house is gone…" Her voice cracked, filled with grief and despair. "How are we going to survive? Have you even thought about our future? Our children?!"

John gazed silently out the window, the endless darkness mirroring the gloom in his heart. After a long pause, he responded in a low, hoarse voice, thick with helplessness and self-reproach. "I don't know, Mina…" He closed his eyes, took a deep breath, and continued with a sigh. "I thought I could control everything, that I could give us a better life. But the truth is, I can't even control my own future."

"Control everything?" Mina's composure shattered, her emotions overflowing like a breached dam, tears streaming down her face. She pointed at John, her hands trembling. "You said you could control everything? And look at us now!" she cried. "We've lost everything! You gambled with our future, and now we can't even keep our home! What were you thinking?! How are we going to survive, John?"

"Mina, I…" John's voice faltered. He wanted to explain but knew his words were useless now. Watching his wife crumble, he felt overwhelmed by guilt and helplessness, as if his entire world were collapsing under the weight of his responsibility. He knew he was the one who had led them into this abyss.

"Have you thought about our children?" Mina's voice was thick with sobs and anger. "What about them? How do you expect me to provide for them?! You didn't even think about us! You were so caught up in your investment dream, like a gambler who lost everything!"

John tried to reach out, to hold her, but his hand froze in midair, held back by an invisible force, all courage draining away. His wife's tears and accusations made him feel small and helpless, as if lost in a dark abyss without hope.

"I'm so sorry, Mina…" John's voice was barely a whisper, hoarse and filled with regret. "I… I just wanted to give us a better life. I thought this was our chance…" His hands fell weakly, as if reaching for vanished dreams and hopes. "But I was wrong; I was so wrong… I didn't know what I was doing…"

"Wrong?! What good is it to say that now?!" Mina cried, her voice raw with despair and anger. "If you had listened to me earlier and not put all our money into those damn stocks, we wouldn't be in this mess! And now? You've made us lose everything! What else do you have to say for yourself? How are we going to face the future? How are we going to raise our children?!"

Mina turned abruptly, burying her face in her hands, her shoulders shaking uncontrollably. Uncontrollable sobs wracked her body, each one a cry of despair.

John stood frozen, unable to move. Every word, every tear was a blow, suffocating him. He couldn't defend himself, nor could he comfort the woman he loved. He hung his head silently, feeling his world crumble around him, his dreams for the future dissolving into regret and remorse.

In that moment, John realized he had lost more than just his wealth; he had lost everything he held dear.

They fell into a long silence, the city lights outside flickering against their exhausted faces. Finally, John broke the silence. "I can't rely on short-term investments anymore," his voice was low but steady. "I know it will be a long process, but we need to start over and rebuild a solid financial foundation."

Mina nodded, a glimmer of hope flickering in her eyes. "What can we do? We have no money left…"

"Mina, there's still a path for us. It will be difficult, but as long as we work hard, there's still hope." John took a deep breath and began to explain their plan of action. "First, we need to sort out all our debts, from the highest to the lowest interest rates. We'll tackle the high-interest ones first to reduce the snowballing effect of interest."

Mina listened intently, nodding in agreement.

"Second, we need to create a strict budget and control our spending. Travel, entertainment, and eating out—all of that is out of the question for now. We may need to move to a cheaper place, even consider selling the car, or parting with any unnecessary belongings to raise cash to pay off our debts."

Mina gently took John's hand, her eyes reflecting a glimmer of hope as she felt his resolve. "I can accept all of that," she said softly, "as long as we're still together. Nothing else matters."

John went on, "We also need to find ways to increase our income. Maybe I can take on part-time jobs or use my expertise to do consulting or investment analysis. Even short-term projects could help us pay down some of our debt. And you... if possible, maybe you could take on freelance work, like writing, translation, or anything else you're good at."

Mina pondered for a moment, then nodded in agreement. "I can try. Maybe I can find some Korean translation work to help support us. It's time for us to work together."

John felt her support, and a warmth spread through him. He knew the road ahead wouldn't be easy, but Mina's understanding and companionship gave him immense strength. He gently squeezed her hand, his eyes filled with gratitude. "Mina, thank you. After all this, you're still willing to stand by me."

Mina smiled, tears still glistening in her eyes, but her smile was filled with determination. "We'll get through this, John. As long as we work together, there's nothing we can't overcome."

A few days later, John met with the Smiths at a dimly lit café, the somber atmosphere mirroring their despair. The Smiths looked exhausted, their faces etched with worry, as if bearing an unbearable burden.

"John, what should we do?" Mrs. Smith asked tearfully. "Our children's dreams of college are shattered. Is there any way out of this?"

John lowered his head, feeling their pain. "I don't know. We all underestimated the risk, overly confident that tech stocks would keep rising… but we have to start over."

The Smiths exchanged a look of doubt and unease. "Can we really get back on our feet? After such a huge loss, do we still have a chance?"

John took a deep breath and shared his and Mina's plan, hoping to offer them a glimmer of hope. "I understand how you feel because we're in the same boat. We've lost all our savings, even our house… but Mina and I have decided to start over. We've made a plan—maybe you could consider it too."

The Smiths looked at each other, hesitant about starting over.

"Our first step," John explained, "is to organize our debts, list them from the highest to the lowest interest rate, and prioritize paying off the high-interest ones first. This will reduce our interest burden and prevent the debt from snowballing. Then, we'll cut all unnecessary expenses. Travel and entertainment—those are out of the question for now. We may need to move to a cheaper place and even consider selling the car or extra belongings to raise cash to pay off our debts."

Mr. Smith lowered his head and murmured, "Do we really have to make such sacrifices…?"

John nodded. "Yes, it will be tough, but we have no other choice. We also plan to increase our income. I'll look for part-time jobs or short-term consulting opportunities, and Mina plans to do some translation work. Maybe you could consider finding temporary jobs too. Even a temporary income can help alleviate the pressure."

Mrs. Smith wiped the tears from the corners of her eyes and asked thoughtfully, "Do you think we really still have a chance?"

John looked at them, his voice firm and sincere. "Yes, we've lost a lot, but the only thing we can't lose is hope and the courage to act. We may not be able to return to our previous lives right away, but as long as we work together, gradually repay our debts, cut expenses, and find opportunities to increase our income, we can get out of this. The important thing is that we learn how to face risks and not make the same mistakes again."

A flicker of trust emerged on the Smiths' exhausted faces, and they seemed to be accepting John's suggestions. Mr. Smith said softly, "You're right, John. We have to stand up and not let this failure defeat us."

John gave them an understanding smile and reached out to shake Mr. Smith's hand. "We've all been through a lot, but this is just a part of our lives, not the end. We can start over, beginning today, step by step, out of this darkness."

The Smiths nodded in agreement, a glimmer of hope dawning on their faces.

Market Reflections

As the market bubble burst, Moorman Investment Group descended into unprecedented chaos. The once bustling and lively office was now suffused with panic. Computer screens flickered with alarming red numbers, stock prices plummeting like free-falling objects. Employees rushed between desks, desperately trying to salvage precarious investment projects. Phones rang incessantly, mostly delivering disheartening news. Investors withdrew their funds, partners severed ties, and the entire company teetered on the brink of collapse.

The atmosphere in the conference room was stifling, the management team's faces ashen, their eyes filled with helplessness and fear. Williams struggled to speak, his voice hoarse, as if all hope had been extinguished. "Moorman can't sustain itself any longer… We've filed for bankruptcy." His words struck like a hammer blow, plunging the room into a deathly silence. Only the ticking of the clock on the wall could be heard, counting down the company's final moments.

As John gathered the documents on his desk, his hands trembled slightly, as if trying to grasp something irretrievable. The proposals that once symbolized the future now seemed worthless, like scraps of paper. He stood by the office window, gazing at the bustling streets of New York below. The contrast between the vibrant city and the ruin within him was stark. At that moment, he felt utterly disconnected from the city—a lost soul, isolated and helpless.

Amidst the chaos and despair, John had to face reality: he had lost his job and his livelihood; his past confidence in the market had transformed into deep regret and doubt. The bursting of the dot-com bubble was a wake-up call, a stark reminder of the dangers of market mania and his own past naiveté. This disaster forced him to re-examine his investment philosophy and recognize that while market frenzy drove prices up, it also masked the accumulation of hidden risks.

This catastrophe forced him to confront the fact that irrational market exuberance would eventually return to rationality. It was precisely when everyone believed the market would only go up that the risk was greatest.

He began to reflect: Why had he been so easily seduced by the market's glamour? Why hadn't he remained clear-headed when the market was swept up in a frenzy? He realized he had been too focused on short-term profits, neglecting the looming risks. In optimistic markets, investors easily get caught up in the herd mentality, driving prices ever higher, even without solid fundamental support. Once market sentiment shifts, panic spreads rapidly, triggering a cascade of sell-offs.

John understood that this panic selling showed how irrational the market could be. Whether in excessive optimism or extreme pessimism, prices could become distorted by emotions. Now, he saw this clearly and was determined not to repeat his mistakes.

During this low point, John revisited the fundamentals of investing. He delved into the works of investment masters like Warren Buffett and Benjamin Graham, reconstructing his investment philosophy. He no longer viewed investing as a tool for quick riches but as an art requiring insight, discipline, and patience for long-term growth.

John turned his attention to undervalued stocks. He believed these companies, despite their current underperformance, held the potential for substantial long-term returns. He began to prioritize risk management, setting stop-loss points, diversifying investments, and placing capital preservation at the core of his strategy.

Weeks later, as John prepared for a job interview, he received a short but hopeful letter from Richard: "We have a new plan. Let's talk."

One afternoon, John, Richard, and Katherine gathered in a small conference room in New York. Richard spoke first, his voice firm and filled with anticipation. "John, we were all saddened by Moorman's fate, but this is not the end. We plan to start a new company called 'Phoenix Investments,' symbolizing rebirth from ashes. We want you to join us and build this new beginning together."

Katherine continued with a smile. "John, this isn't just our idea; we have the support of several key clients from Moorman. They have great confidence in our new plan and are willing to invest to help us launch this project. They value our expertise and past experience and believe this is a worthwhile investment opportunity."

She paused, her tone becoming more sincere. "This is a rare opportunity for us to start over and allow those who once trusted us to continue believing in our abilities. We hope you'll join us and create this new chapter together."

John was surprised, looking up at Richard and Katherine. "I'm honored by the invitation, but starting a business... that's a big risk. We're short on funds, market confidence is low, and investors are wary of the financial industry right now."

Katherine nodded with a smile. "Yes, John, we're well aware of the challenges. But that's precisely why we need you. You've weathered this storm and know how to calmly analyze risks. We're no longer chasing short-term profits; we're focused on long-term value investing, especially in companies with a strong sense of social responsibility."

John pondered the concept. "Long-term value investing… that means we need to avoid market hype and focus on finding companies with real potential. But to do so, our selection criteria must be strict, and we'll need to have enough confidence."

"Exactly," Richard picked up the thread. "We don't intend to repeat our past mistakes. We'll pay close attention to the company's fundamentals and strengthen our risk management. This time, we're building a stable institution focused on long-term value creation."

Katherine added, "We also need to build trust with our clients, so investors know we're a responsible company focused on long-term growth, not an institution that profits from speculation."

John's eyes grew more determined. This was more than just a career opportunity; it was a chance to redefine himself. "If we can overcome these challenges, I believe we can succeed. I agree with your direction.

This time, we'll move forward with more caution and rationality."

As John left the meeting room and walked down the bustling streets of New York, his mind swirled with excitement and apprehension, the magnitude of his choice weighing heavily upon him. The thought of building Phoenix Investments from the ground up filled him with a sense of purpose he hadn't felt in a long time. Yet, beneath that excitement lay a lingering unease, a reminder of the risks and sacrifices ahead. Each step he took echoed his doubts, amplifying the pressure of this new beginning. On his way home, he grappled with how to discuss this life-altering decision with Mina, hoping she would understand the importance of this second chance, yet fearing the worry it might stir in her heart.

When he arrived home, Mina was sitting on the sofa reading. She looked up when John walked in and smiled, "How did the interview go?"

Setting down his bag, John sat beside her and took a deep breath, hesitation coloring his voice as he began to speak. "Actually, things went a bit differently today. Richard and Katherine invited me to join their new company—'Phoenix Investments.' They have a solid vision and want to rebuild a more stable investment firm."

Mina frowned slightly and gently set down her book. Concern was evident in her eyes. "Starting a business? John, we've already faced so much risk. Isn't this too risky? We've only just stabilized. Are you sure this is the best choice?"

John knew how important this opportunity was, though her concern made his heart tighten. "I know this decision might seem a little crazy," he said, trying to stay calm, "but this time is different. This isn't just about starting a business—it's a chance to rebuild myself and fix past mistakes. I can't let us fall into the same traps again. I've learned a lot, and I know how to handle the risks now."

Mina gazed deeply into his eyes, the internal conflict evident in her expression. "I understand that you want to get back on your feet, but our finances have just started to stabilize. Are you sure this won't spiral out of control like last time?" Her voice quivered with anxiety, reflecting the unease in her heart.

Sensing her worry, John knew he needed to be more cautious this time. He took her hand, his eyes filled with sincerity and determination. "Mina, I swear I won't be impulsive this time. I've learned how to protect our assets. This opportunity is different—Richard and Katherine have also gone through similar setbacks. We all share the same goal: stable growth, focused on long-term value investing. I won't take unnecessary risks. I'll be careful; I promise."

Mina's expression softened slightly, though there was still a trace of doubt in her eyes. "So, you really believe this is our opportunity?"

John nodded, his voice firm. "Yes. This time, I'm not chasing short-term gains. I want to build a company that's truly responsible and can bring long-term returns, both for us and our clients. This is a chance for rebirth—not just for my career but for our life together."

Mina let out a soft sigh. Though there was still some lingering concern in her heart, John's determination and sincerity slowly eased her worries. She knew that after all they had been through, he was no longer the man who could be easily swayed by market glitz. She reached out, gently touching his face, her voice tender. "Alright, John. If you truly believe this is our chance, I'll support you. I just want you to remember that, no matter the outcome, we're in this together."

John felt a wave of warmth flow through him. Looking deeply into Mina's eyes, he felt the pressure in his chest lighten. "Thank you, Mina. I know that this time we'll move forward more cautiously, together." He embraced her, feeling her support bolster his resolve.

This conversation cemented John's determination. He knew that no matter what challenges lay ahead, as long as Mina was by his side, he had the strength to face them. In that moment, he made his decision—he was ready to join Richard and Katherine and face the challenges ahead with Phoenix Investments. Together, they would start a new chapter for themselves and their family.

With the establishment of Phoenix Investments, they faced numerous difficulties. A shortage of funds and a lack of trust from investors made the company's early days tough. But just when things seemed bleak, an unexpected opportunity arose.

To combat the economic recession brought on by the dot-com bubble collapse, the U.S. government decided to create the "National Recovery Fund," aimed at stimulating economic growth through investment. The fund's capital primarily came from government appropriations and public donations, with targeted investments in sectors such as technology, energy, and healthcare—all with strong long-term growth potential.

Richard and Katherine, seeing the opportunity, decided to compete for the management rights to the National Recovery Fund. They believed this would be a key catalyst for Phoenix Investments' rapid rise. After a fierce competition, Phoenix Investments successfully won the rights to manage this crucial fund.

When news of the National Recovery Fund's establishment broke, Phoenix Investments immediately recognized it as a rare opportunity. However, the competition for the fund's management rights was fierce, with many well-known investment firms eager to gain control of this significant financial resource. Richard, Katherine, and John knew that this would be a hard-fought battle.

They acted quickly, crafting a detailed proposal that highlighted Phoenix Investments' long-term development strategy and its commitment to social responsibility. The proposal not only emphasized their investment philosophy but also showcased their strengths in risk management and sustainable development. They understood that, compared to larger investment firms, Phoenix Investments was at a disadvantage in terms of size and resources, so they decided to differentiate themselves by focusing on innovation and responsibility.

However, their competitors weren't going to back down easily. Large investment firms, backed by their considerable financial resources and strong track records, presented compelling forecasts of potential investment returns. Though Phoenix Investments was a newcomer, Richard and John knew that their strength lay in their deep understanding of the market and their sharp insight into risk.

During a high-stakes bidding meeting organized by senior government officials, John stood at the podium, ready to deliver a critical proposal. The atmosphere in the room was tense, with competitors' eyes fixed on him, the weight of anticipation pressing down. Yet, John remained composed. His speech didn't dwell on short-term gains but focused instead on a strategy for long-term, stable growth. He stressed that the purpose of the recovery fund was not just to secure quick profits but to establish a sustainable foundation for the nation's future economy.

"We aim not only to provide an immediate boost to economic recovery but also to ensure that the industries we invest in can grow over the long term, creating stable employment opportunities and fostering innovation. We believe that by prioritizing companies with a strong sense of social responsibility and sustainable development projects, this fund can deliver true value to the nation, rather than simply chasing short-term financial returns," John said with calm confidence.

When John concluded his speech, the room fell silent. The government officials in attendance seemed deep in thought, clearly reflecting on the stark contrast between Phoenix Investments' proposal and those of its competitors.

In the days that followed, Richard and Katherine worked tirelessly, maintaining communication with the government's review committee. They addressed concerns, clarified Phoenix Investments' strategy, and underscored their unique advantages. Despite mounting pressure from larger competitors, they stayed focused and composed.

Finally, the government made its decision—Phoenix Investments had won the management rights to the National Recovery Fund.

For Phoenix Investments, this news was a beacon of hope, symbolizing rebirth and opportunity. Though this victory was just the first step, John knew that the challenges ahead would be even greater. But he was more convinced than ever that this time, they wouldn't be chasing short-term profits. Instead, they would blend rationality, responsibility, and long-term growth to create lasting value, both for their company and for the nation.

THE AGE OF STORMS: JOHN REYNOLDS' FINANCIAL STRUGGLE

CHAPTER 4

THE FINANCIAL TSUNAMI 2008

The Hidden Risks of Subprime Mortgages

The bursting of the dot-com bubble in 2000 plunged the American economy into a recession. By the first quarter of 2001, economic contraction was evident, with global economic activity slowing and international trade volumes declining. The collapse of the tech bubble led to the shutdown of numerous technology companies, pushing up the unemployment rate, particularly in the tech sector. Investor confidence in the technology industry was severely shaken, and both venture capital funding and the number of IPOs (initial public offerings) dropped sharply, leaving the market in a state of malaise.

To revive the economy, the Federal Reserve began a cycle of interest rate cuts in 2001, drastically lowering rates to historic lows. This policy fueled rapid growth in the real estate market, with property prices soaring steadily. As demand in the housing market surged, banks and financial institutions began loosening credit standards, extending loans to borrowers with lower credit ratings. These high-risk loans, known as "subprime loans," carried higher interest rates than traditional loans, generating lucrative profits for financial institutions. However, these profits concealed enormous risks.

During this housing boom, Phoenix Investments capitalized on the government's "National Recovery Fund," making a series of strategic investments that yielded impressive returns. As the fund's investment manager, John led the team to great success amidst the real estate frenzy, and the company grew significantly. As his achievements accumulated, John gradually became a sought-after investment guru in the industry.

However, in 2006, John began to feel a growing sense of unease. He witnessed the frenzied growth of the real estate market, with housing prices rising far beyond the pace of income growth. He knew that if this irrational exuberance reversed, it would trigger an unavoidable collapse. John's contemplation was interrupted by the arrival of Kevin Rogers, a sharp, newly recruited member of the Phoenix Investments team.

John's office occupied the corner of a skyscraper, its floor-to-ceiling windows overlooking the entire city. In the distance, high-rise buildings and streams of traffic looked like miniature models arranged within the city's frame. His desk was neatly organized with various financial reports and market analysis charts, while the dark walnut bookshelf displayed classic finance books. An abstract painting hung on the wall, seemingly hinting at the complexity and capriciousness of the market.

Kevin strode in, dressed in a dark blue suit with a maroon tie, his overall appearance refined yet professional. His expression was determined, and his eyes radiated confidence. Without hesitation, he sat down opposite John, his hands folded in his lap, exuding an air of assurance.

"You seem rather cautious about the market lately," Kevin said directly, not hiding his wariness.

John sat in his spacious leather chair, gently twirling the pen in his hand, his gaze shifting from the skyscrapers outside the window back to the documents in front of him. "Yes, the real estate market is so hot right now; I feel things have gone out of control." His tone was calm, but worry flickered in his eyes.

Kevin pulled a thick report from his briefcase and quickly handed it to John. "I was just thinking about discussing this with you. This is my recent analysis of the subprime mortgage market. The situation is worse than we anticipated."

John's brow furrowed as he skimmed through the report, the tip of his pen tapping lightly on the desk as if pondering the implications behind each number and phrase. "These loans are being given to people with unstable credit?"

"Exactly," Kevin responded swiftly, anxiety creeping into his voice while maintaining a professional calm. "Many borrowers don't have stable incomes. Their loans are entirely based on the assumption that housing prices will continue to rise. If prices fall, these people won't be able to repay their loans."

"That's a huge risk for financial institutions," John said softly, his expression turning serious.

"Worse, the subprime market is expanding rapidly," Kevin added. "If this bubble bursts, the consequences will be unimaginable."

John stared at the inverted yield curve on his computer screen, alarm bells clanging in his mind. He recalled the painful lessons of the 2000 dot-com bubble, and this time, he was determined not to let the crisis escalate. He promptly began formulating a plan to gradually reduce Phoenix Investments' exposure as the market heated up, carefully timing his actions to avoid sudden impacts on the price. Rather than making drastic moves, John aimed to slowly unwind their positions in subprime-related assets while the demand remained high. He also considered buying Credit Default Swaps (CDS) as a precautionary hedge against potential losses, preparing for the possibility of an eventual downturn. Yet, John remained vigilant, meticulously monitoring market conditions and waiting for the right moment to execute his strategy fully.

As John began to deploy risk-hedging measures, investors in the market remained enthralled by the real estate boom. They believed that housing prices would only continue to rise, and the allure of high returns from subprime mortgages attracted a flood of capital. Investment institutions packaged these high-risk loans into financial products, selling them rapidly, while investors eagerly snapped them up as if it were a never-ending feast.

A few days later, at Phoenix Investments' headquarters, a crucial meeting on the company's strategy was underway. The atmosphere in the conference room was calm and focused, with electronic screens on the walls displaying various data on the real estate market and subprime mortgages. Katherine, dressed in a dark gray suit, stood at the end of the conference table, her voice steady and decisive. "Today, our focus is on how to respond to the current real estate market. We need to re-evaluate our investment direction, especially the risks in the subprime mortgage market."

John shifted his gaze from the data to Katherine, his voice calm and firm as he opened the report in front of him. "I think we should immediately reduce our holdings of subprime-related assets. The market bubble is evident; the rise in housing prices is detached from the fundamentals of the real economy."

Katherine nodded, her gaze fixed on John. "Do you have any specific suggestions?"

John continued, "The yield curve has inverted. This is a very clear warning sign. Based on past experience, we know this is usually a precursor to a recession. Reducing our subprime assets now and hedging the risk by buying Credit Default Swaps (CDS) is the wisest choice."

Katherine listened attentively, a thoughtful nod

confirming her understanding. "I think your concerns are well-founded. That's why we chose you to be the investment manager for this fund. I trust your judgment, especially at this critical moment." She looked around at the other senior members. "We will proceed according to John's suggestion, reduce our subprime assets, and initiate the risk hedging plan. Our focus should be on long-term stability, not short-term gains."

Richard Harkins, seated on the other side of the conference table, had a flicker of doubt in his eyes but didn't strongly object. "Since Katherine agrees, I respect the decision. We must carefully consider every risk."

Katherine added, "Risk management is at the core of investing. We need to ensure that the company's assets are under control in all circumstances. The decisions made in this meeting are based on our prudent analysis of the current market situation. I believe John will lead us safely through this risky period."

One afternoon, John picked up the ringing phone to hear Steve's anxious voice filling the receiver. Since the collapse of Moorman Investments, Steve had moved to Lehman Brothers.

"John, you're being far too conservative!" Steve said impatiently. "The market is surging right now. This is your chance to make a killing, and you're missing out!"

John frowned slightly, maintaining his composure. "Steve, our goal isn't to maximize short-term profits but to achieve long-term, stable growth."

"Long-term stability?" Steve said with a scoff. "Now is the perfect time to make a fortune. If we don't get in now, we're missing out on a once-in-a-lifetime opportunity!"

"Often, when the market seems strongest, that's when the greatest risks are hidden," John countered calmly. "Our priority is to protect our assets, not to be blinded by temporary prosperity."

Steve was silent for a moment, then his voice rose with agitation. "A conservative strategy will make you miss all the opportunities. This is the best time the market has offered us, and I don't think we should let it slip away."

John remained calm, replying evenly, " time will prove whose decision is right."

Despite the market frenzy and ridicule, John remained steadfast. He knew his judgment shouldn't be based on short-term market fluctuations but on a long-term assessment of risk. "When the market seems strongest, that's often when the greatest risks are hidden," he told his team. "Our priority is to protect our assets, not to be blinded by temporary prosperity."

One afternoon, John was reviewing market data in his office, his brow furrowed. Suddenly, Richard burst in, his voice urgent and his face etched with anxiety. "John, Bear Stearns' subprime hedge funds are in serious trouble!"

"What happened?" John immediately stopped what he was doing and looked up.

"Two of their subprime funds have suffered heavy losses and are now facing liquidation." Richard shook his head. "This is Bear Stearns, a Wall Street giant, and they've stumbled into the subprime quagmire."

"I can't believe it," Katherine said, joining the conversation with a frown. "If even Bear Stearns can't avoid this crisis, what about other institutions? This is definitely not an isolated incident."

John leaned back in his chair, his thoughts churning.

"We saw the signs early on. Bear Stearns is just the first giant to fall. The real crisis has just begun."

"Yes, the risks in the subprime market have already spread," Katherine said calmly. "If even Bear Stearns can't escape unscathed, the entire market will face a huge impact."

"That's what I've been worried about." John took a deep breath, his voice firm. "We must immediately strengthen our response measures and reduce our exposure to all risk assets."

Richard paced back and forth, looking agitated. "I have to admit, I was too optimistic about the market before, but now I understand that your caution was right."

"It's time to take action." John stood up, his eyes determined. "We need to protect our assets and guide the team through this storm."

"Doing the right thing is often the hardest, but that's our responsibility." Katherine patted Richard's shoulder, her voice filled with determination.

Richard nodded silently, knowing that the storm was inevitable. Only John's decisions could lead them through this crisis.

The Crisis Unfolds

In the summer of 2008, news of Lehman Brothers teetering on the brink of bankruptcy spread across Wall Street like a virus, triggering a wave of market turmoil. The stock market plummeted as soon as it opened, with the three major U.S. indices—the Dow Jones Industrial Average, the S&P 500, and the Nasdaq—each dropping more than 5% within just one hour. Investor panic swept across Wall Street. The market resembled a dance on the edge of a knife, with countless company stocks plunging in free fall, seemingly without an end in sight.

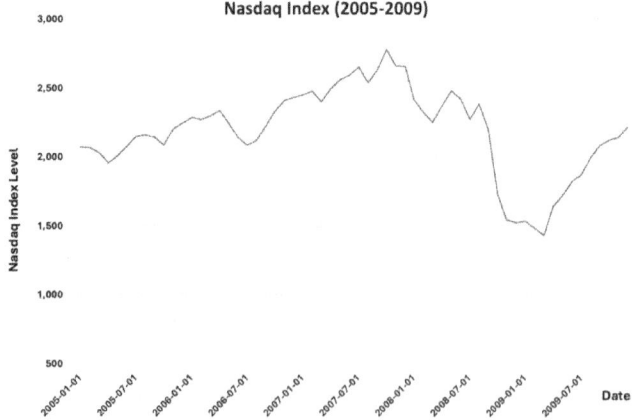

The chart shows the fluctuation of the Nasdaq Index from 2005 to 2009, with a significant decline in 2008 following the global financial crisis. This event had a profound impact on the U.S. economy and financial markets, leading to a sharp drop in stock prices.
Source of data: Federal Reserve Economic Data, FRED.

Inside the trading floor of Phoenix Investments, the usual hustle and bustle had been replaced by a tense silence. Flashing red numbers dominated every screen, and the faces of the traders were etched with anxiety and unease. The once-frantic ringing of phones had become sparse, replaced by an oppressive quiet.

Katherine hurried into the trading room, her expression grim and her voice low. "Lehman Brothers' situation is worsening. The market has become extremely volatile."

John's brow furrowed as his eyes remained glued to the screen. The market's downturn was far swifter and more severe than he had anticipated. "This is the storm we foresaw," he murmured. "Lehman is just the beginning. We need to reduce our risk exposure immediately, or the situation will spiral out of control."

Richard joined the conversation, his voice calm but tinged with tension. "Financial stocks are extremely risky. We need to reduce our holdings across the board in any financial institution with significant exposure to subprime mortgages, especially those on the verge of collapse, like Lehman."

"Absolutely," Katherine responded instantly. "And

not just financial stocks. We need to quickly liquidate any high-risk assets related to real estate as well."

John stood up, his expression focused and decisive. "We need to do everything we can to protect our capital, ensure stable cash flow, and minimize our risk exposure as much as possible."

Katherine's brow furrowed. "But market liquidity is drying up fast. How long can our cash flow last?"

Richard narrowed his eyes, considering the situation. "The government won't just sit back and watch. A bailout plan will likely be announced soon."

John's gaze remained serious. "We can't rely on external rescues. We have to manage the risk ourselves. All high-risk assets must be liquidated immediately. That's the only thing we can control."

He paused, then called out to Kevin, "Kevin, immediately list the high-risk assets we need to prioritize for selling, especially those financial institutions linked to real estate and subprime mortgages, particularly those with severe liquidity issues."

Kevin nodded without hesitation. "We should start

with the companies that have the worst liquidity. Those assets have been ticking time bombs waiting to explode. I'll get right on it."

"Which ones do you think are the riskiest right now?" John asked, seeking Kevin's professional opinion.

Kevin didn't miss a beat, his fingers flying across the keyboard as he responded. "Those with excessive exposure to subprime mortgages, like Countrywide Financial, have capital structures that are too fragile. With the current market conditions, they won't last long."

"Once the list is ready, sell them on the market immediately," John said firmly. "Every minute is critical. We have to clear out all risk assets before the market collapses further."

Kevin glanced at John, a hint of challenge in his voice. "We need to move even faster. We should have already sold these. This is the most dangerous time. The market is crashing faster than we anticipated."

John nodded. "I know time is of the essence, but we have to make sure every step is accurate."

Kevin's fingers flew across the keyboard. "I'll finish as soon as possible. We're racing against time. If we act quickly enough, we can still clear these assets before the market completely collapses."

However, the market was unraveling faster than anyone expected. The daily declines in the stock market grew larger, with financial stocks being hit the hardest. Investors scrambled to sell, and panic engulfed Wall Street. Liquidity rapidly dried up, and even basic financing channels began to clog.

Katherine re-entered the office, her expression anxious. "We've significantly reduced our risk exposure, but market liquidity has nearly evaporated. If this continues, we won't be able to meet our cash flow needs."

John calmly added, "The liquidity crunch means almost no one is willing to buy assets. The market is completely out of balance, and this will only further fuel the panic."

He pondered for a moment, his voice steady but alert. "We have to prepare for the worst. The market is no longer following any normal rules. Every step we take must be precisely calculated to ensure the fund's survival through this storm."

As the market turmoil intensified, John knew this crisis was just the beginning. The challenges ahead would be even more daunting, but he understood that the fate of Phoenix Investments rested on their every decision and action.

The Collapse of the Global Economy

On Monday morning, September 15, 2008, a cold rain lashed the windows of New York's skyscrapers, mirroring the unmistakable sense of unease that permeated the market. On the trading floor of Phoenix Investments, tension was palpable. **On the television screen, a CNN anchor was broadcasting news that would shock the world: "Lehman Brothers files for bankruptcy protection!"**

The news ripped through the trading floor like a shockwave. Traders stopped in their tracks, anxiety filling their eyes. The stock market plummeted immediately after opening, triggering circuit breakers repeatedly. Traders fell into chaos, frantically checking market data and unable to cope with the sudden disaster.

"The collapse of Lehman Brothers marks the worst financial crisis since the Great Depression," the anchor's voice echoed through the office. The screen showed the streets of New York, where investors paced anxiously while Lehman executives tried to dodge the media's cameras. The Lehman Brothers building loomed in the footage, a towering giant on the verge of collapse, sending chills down everyone's spine.

Lehman's collapse triggered a global financial storm, like a line of falling dominoes. The market plunged into unprecedented turbulence, swallowing everything like a vortex. The office lights felt cold and harsh, reflecting the mounting pressure within.

John took a deep breath, his hands trembling slightly from long-term stress as he struggled to maintain his composure. Although he had anticipated the storm, the scene unfolding before him still felt overwhelming. He turned around, slowly adjusting his suit to appear more composed, despite the inner turmoil. In an emergency meeting, his voice remained steady and firm: "Everyone's worried, but we can't lose our heads. We've prepared for this, and our risk exposure is much lower than that of other companies. We must trust our strategy; we will survive this crisis."

He scanned everyone's faces, searching for a flicker of confidence in their eyes.

Richard stood nearby, arms crossed, brow furrowed, his eyes reflecting exhaustion and worry. "This disaster is just beginning," he muttered, his gaze fixed on the flickering image of the Lehman Brothers building on the screen. His voice was subdued, but the unmistakable fear in his eyes added to the weight of the moment.

Catherine stood by the conference table, arms folded, shaking her head slightly. Though her voice remained calm, there was clear anxiety beneath the surface. "We may have avoided the worst of this crisis," she spoke slowly and cautiously, "but I'm worried about the chain reaction in the market. If everyone starts panic selling, liquidity will quickly dry up, and we might not be able to sell in time." Her brow furrowed, and her eyes were filled with a mix of fear and helplessness.

John nodded in agreement, pondering for a moment as the pressure weighed heavily on him. He turned toward the door. "Kevin, come in for a moment."

Kevin quickly entered the room, his steps steady

but slightly hurried, his eyes showing a hint of anxiety, though his tightly pressed lips revealed his effort to remain calm. John addressed him: "I need you to keep a close watch on the market, especially on liquidity. Report any unusual movements to me immediately."

Kevin nodded quickly and sat down. His fingers flew over the keyboard, his eyes fixed on the screen. His heart raced in sync with the market's movements. Though his anxiety simmered beneath the surface, his hands remained steady, each number reminding him of the urgency of time.

"Catherine is right," John continued, his tone calm but betraying the growing anxiety within. "We need to prepare for the worst. I'll reach out to our counterparties to see if we can swap some of our low-liquidity assets. That could boost our liquidity position."

Just as the discussion started, another major news story flashed across the TV screen: **"Fannie Mae and Freddie Mac were taken over by the U.S. government earlier this month. These two enterprises control nearly half of the U.S. mortgage market. The spread of the subprime crisis has overwhelmed them…"**

John listened quietly, his frown deepening. He had foreseen the severity of the crisis, but it was clearly spiraling beyond even his expectations.

"This isn't just about Lehman Brothers," he said softly, "the entire financial system is collapsing. This is a global storm."

As he contemplated the next course of action, the TV screen switched to news of Washington Mutual's collapse.

"Washington Mutual, the largest savings and loan association in the U.S., was taken over by the Federal Deposit Insurance Corporation yesterday, marking the largest bank failure in U.S. history…"

Catherine's eyes widened as she turned to John, her voice filled with concern. "This crisis is spreading across the entire financial system. It could affect all our investment areas next."

Richard gripped his pen tightly, his tone grave: "The panic in the market has spiraled out of control. Stocks are in free fall. While our hedging strategy has reduced some risk, this storm won't end anytime soon."

"Indeed," John nodded slowly, speaking heavily,

"we've significantly reduced our risk exposure, but now the most important thing is to keep a close eye on liquidity and ensure that our capital survives this storm."

Amid their discussion, the television screen flashed with news of AIG's troubles.

"One of the world's largest insurance companies—AIG—is in a financial crisis," the screen displayed details of the U.S. government's rescue plan. "The U.S. government took control of AIG on September 16th with a rescue package worth $85 billion."

Catherine's expression shifted slightly, her voice tinged with anxiety. "If even a company like AIG needs a government bailout, what could possibly be safe?"

John paused for a moment before responding calmly, "There's no safe harbor in this crisis; no one is immune. But our advantage lies in the fact that we saw the risks coming and prepared for them."

Days later, Catherine gathered John and Richard for an emergency meeting to evaluate their next steps.

"We reduced our exposure to high-risk subprime-related assets early on, which puts us in a relatively favorable position," Catherine said, her tone slightly relieved but still cautious.

"Indeed," John remarked, reviewing the market report. "We've avoided the worst losses, but the market remains unstable. We need to maintain adequate cash flow and start looking for quality assets at low prices to position ourselves for the future. The greater the turbulence, the more opportunities arise."

Richard nodded in agreement. "This is the best time to position ourselves for the future, but every step must be cautious and precise. Market uncertainty remains extremely high; we can't let our guard down."

John walked to the window, gazing at New York's skyline through the glass, contemplating each upcoming decision. "No one can escape this storm, but our mission isn't just to survive—it's to find opportunities for rebirth in the chaos." He turned to face the team, his eyes resolute. "Every decision from here on is crucial. We must stay highly vigilant and calculate each risk and opportunity with precision."

Catherine nodded in response. "We'll continue closely monitoring market changes and looking for undervalued quality assets. When the market stabilizes, we'll be in a strong position."

"Exactly," Richard added. "In this crisis, the ultimate winners will be those investors who stay calm and keep a long-term vision. This is our chance."

Their discussion was filled with tension and determination. Everyone understood that this financial storm would fundamentally change the market landscape, but it would also create new opportunities. Phoenix Investment Company, true to its name, would need to rise from the ashes.

As the meeting concluded, John, Catherine, and Richard returned to their posts to continue monitoring the market. They knew that every decision moving forward would determine the company's fate after this financial storm.

As the global financial crisis spread, the real economy suffered severe damage. U.S. Gross Domestic Product (GDP) fell by 8.4% in the fourth quarter of 2008, the largest decline since 1982. Global manufacturing, services, and trade systems were hit hard, and economic activity nearly ground to a halt. Companies began mass layoffs, unemployment rates surged across nations, and the U.S. unemployment rate peaked at 10% in October 2009.

The Wave of Foreclosures and Broken Families

The subprime mortgage crisis dealt a devastating blow to the American people, leaving a trail of shattered dreams and broken homes in its wake. Thousands of families were unable to make their mortgage payments, and foreclosures swept across the nation. Housing prices collapsed, and countless people lost their homes. Many were forced to leave their familiar residences for cheap rentals, while others ended up on the streets.

One evening, John met Eric at a coffee shop, his friend's expression weary and his eyes filled with concern after returning from reporting in one of the hardest-hit cities.

"It's really bad," Eric said, placing his notebook on the table, his brow furrowed. "I just got back from Cleveland, and what I saw was heartbreaking. Entire neighborhoods are almost empty, houses are foreclosed, and homeless people are everywhere. Many don't even know where to go."

"I interviewed some people who lost their homes,"

Eric continued, his voice trembling slightly. "There was a single mother with two children who had been living in her car for over a month. She said she didn't know what to do or where to go."

Eric paused, taking a long sip of coffee, as if trying to wash away the images he had witnessed. "Then there was an elderly man who lost his house and all his savings. Now he's surviving on government assistance. He said he never imagined he'd end up like this."

John nodded, his expression grim. "This crisis goes far beyond the financial markets. It's destroying countless families."

Eric sighed, wearily rubbing his forehead. "This isn't just about foreclosures anymore—it's a social crisis. Families are breaking apart, marriages are failing, and children have nowhere to go. Government assistance programs haven't been implemented yet, and things are only getting worse."

After a moment of silence, John spoke slowly: "This is something our generation has never seen before. The global economy is deep in recession, and the entire system is crumbling. All we can do is continue monitoring the market and make sure our strategies can weather this storm."

That night, when John returned home, Mina was anxiously watching the news on the couch. The screen showed reports about the wave of foreclosures.

"How long will this crisis last?" Mina asked, her voice filled with worry. "So many people have lost their homes. What should we do?"

John gazed out at the city lights through the window, speaking softly: "We've avoided the worst losses, but we can't let our guard down. The global economy is entering a deep recession—something we've never experienced before."

"What should we do?" Mina gently squeezed his hand, seeking reassurance.

"We've adjusted our investment strategy, and our cash flow is relatively stable, but the future of the market is full of uncertainty," John said firmly but cautiously. "We need to be prepared for the long haul and remain prudent. This crisis won't end quickly, but we'll get through it."

A few days later, John called Kevin into his office; his colleague's face was etched with exhaustion and anxiety.

"The market's getting worse," Kevin said as soon as he entered, his brow furrowed. "Waves of selling keep coming. We're forced to follow the market's movements, like an avalanche that won't stop."

John nodded silently, his gaze solemn as he looked out the window. "Every sale feels like pouring oil on the fire, speeding up the collapse."

"Can we stop selling?" Kevin sighed, tiredly rubbing his forehead. "Investors are panicking. No one wants to wait until the market completely crashes before pulling out. We have no way out."

"We have a responsibility to protect our investors' assets," John said quietly. "But each sale risks triggering a chain reaction, pushing the market lower."

Kevin frowned, lightly tapping the desk. "The market is like a teetering building, and our hedging strategies are only shaking it further. The scariest part is that no one knows when it will collapse."

John sighed heavily, his voice filled with helplessness. "Our hedging strategies can't stop the crash; they can only minimize the damage."

Kevin lowered his voice, a shadow crossing his eyes: "Have we become accomplices in this crisis? We know where the market is heading, but we can't just stand by."

John stared at Kevin, conflicted. "We're part of this system. No matter how cautious we are, the system is already full of cracks. All we can do is try to survive the storm."

The atmosphere in the room grew heavier. The television screen switched to a news report, the anchor's voice urgent: "National unemployment rates have hit historic highs, and the number of homeless people is surging, painting a heartbreaking picture."

The scene shifted to city streets, where groups of homeless people gathered near abandoned buildings. A mother held her child, her face marked with exhaustion and helplessness.

John and Kevin exchanged a heavy glance, both weighed down by the gravity of the situation. "This isn't just a financial crisis," John said quietly, sorrow filling his eyes. "This is the collapse of society."

Kevin nodded, his voice filled with resignation. "We're not just witnessing the breakdown of the economic system; we're seeing families and entire communities being torn apart."

The two fell into silence as the images on the television continued to show the far-reaching effects of the disaster.

Market Rescue and Intervention

As the financial crisis spiraled out of control, the U.S. government and Federal Reserve were forced to take emergency measures to prevent the collapse of the entire financial system. On October 3, 2008, Congress swiftly passed the $700 billion Troubled Asset Relief Program (TARP), authorizing the Treasury Department to purchase troubled assets from financial institutions in an attempt to stabilize markets and restore investor confidence.

Subsequently, in November 2008, the Federal Reserve took an unprecedented step by implementing a quantitative easing (QE) policy, initiating large-scale purchases of mortgage-backed securities (MBS) and U.S. Treasury bonds. This measure aimed to lower long-term interest rates, increase credit supply, and inject liquidity into the market. This unprecedented intervention became a critical turning point in the Fed's response to the crisis and marked a significant shift in how central banks globally would address economic recessions.

As one of the few investors who had correctly anticipated the crisis, John and the Phoenix Investment team were invited to participate in implementing TARP. They not only helped clean up troubled assets from financial institutions but also provided risk analysis and asset evaluation to help determine which institutions and assets should receive priority assistance.

"This isn't just about allocating funds. Each of our decisions will have a profound impact on the future of the market," John said during a team meeting. His tone was calm and resolute, fully aware of the immense responsibility they were facing.

As the bailout program progressed, John's expertise earned him high recognition from top officials at the Treasury Department and the Federal Reserve. Their analysis was not only precise but also capable of predicting which companies had recovery potential, making Phoenix Investment a key partner in the TARP program. John's reputation grew rapidly, and he was soon promoted to become one of Phoenix Investment's main partners.

However, John had his sights set on something bigger. He saw even bigger opportunities. As financial stocks plummeted, many high-quality companies became undervalued, creating an ideal entry point. He decided to approach several struggling major banks, offering to improve their capital liquidity through capital injections and option purchases while acquiring large equity stakes at low prices.

"We can provide capital support through investments, but we'll need to conduct thorough evaluations and receive a certain proportion of equity and preferred stock," John proposed during a meeting with executives from a prominent bank.

A thoughtful silence fell over the room as the bank executives considered John's proposal. They couldn't ignore the crisis at hand, but John's proposal was undeniably an excellent solution. For them, it wasn't just about short-term capital relief but also about laying the foundation for future recovery. For John, it was an opportunity to acquire quality equity at bargain prices.

As the crisis intensified, John began gradually

acquiring equity stakes in several major banks and financial institutions. Each move was carefully calculated, with thorough asset evaluations before every transaction to ensure minimal risk and optimal returns.

"This isn't just about bailouts; it's about reconstruction," John told his team. "We're not just helping these financial institutions survive; we're creating long-term value for our investors."

However, these moves were not without pressure. Some team members expressed concerns about John's aggressive positioning, worried about market uncertainty and stock volatility. During one meeting, Kevin couldn't help but ask, "Can we really handle such big risks? If the market keeps deteriorating, our assets will take a serious hit."

John's gaze remained steady as he responded calmly: "Every decision we've made has been carefully evaluated. Crisis brings risks, but it also brings opportunities. We're not just avoiding losses—we're seizing every opportunity the market presents at its lowest points."

Gradually, John's strategy began to bear fruit.

Although the market remained volatile, the financial stocks he had acquired slowly started to recover value, and these long-term positions promised to bring significant returns to Phoenix Investment. John's reputation on Wall Street soared, making him a model of success during the crisis.

"Even in the darkest moments, there is always light," John reminded himself. He knew that every crisis held infinite opportunities, and he understood that future success would be built on every decision made in the present.

This crisis gave John a deeper understanding of the fragility and unpredictability of markets. It also prompted him to reassess the importance of risk management. Together with his team, he summarized their lessons from the crisis and developed more forward-looking investment strategies, ensuring they would be better prepared to protect their assets and seize new growth opportunities before the next wave of market turmoil arrived.

THE AGE OF STORMS: JOHN REYNOLDS'
FINANCIAL STRUGGLE

CHAPTER 5

AFTER THE STORM

Reflecting on the Storm and Understanding Risk

As the financial storm subsided, John sank back into his office chair, exhausted but exhilarated, emotions swirling inside him. He had witnessed both the market's dizzying heights and its devastating collapse. In this storm, countless financial institutions had crumbled overnight, and many investors paid a brutal price for their overleveraged positions.

Late at night, John's office remained brightly lit. He pored over Lehman Brothers' financial statements, as if trying to find the hidden signs of the collapse. Reflecting on the past, he admitted that in his younger years, he had been too focused on short-term returns, blind to the systemic risks lurking in the market. Lehman's collapse and the takeover of Fannie Mae and Freddie Mac each served as a stark reminder that financial crises stemmed not just from market mechanics but from human nature itself. It was the insatiable greed and blind pursuit of short-term gains that ultimately led to disaster.

Over the years, each crisis had reshaped his investment philosophy. He had come to understand that risk management wasn't a hindrance to profit but a protective barrier on the road to long-term success.

Market uncertainty couldn't be entirely predicted, but it could be effectively managed. This financial storm had driven home the importance of vigilant and adaptable risk management as the key to future success.

John thought back to the Gulf War in 1990, when he first entered the financial world. He recalled his initial realization of how deeply geopolitics could influence market volatility. His understanding of the markets had been simplistic at the time, but that experience opened his eyes to the inseparable connection between global economics and politics, laying the foundation for his awareness of risk.

Then came the 1997 Asian Financial Crisis, where John witnessed the devastating impact of leverage. He saw the helplessness of Southeast Asian nations in the face of capital flight, with the collapse of market confidence hitting the entire region hard. This experience taught him about the power of liquidity and market sentiment, and how quickly a crisis could unfold with overwhelming force.

The dot-com bubble of 2000 was another pivotal moment in John's life. Amid the tech stock frenzy, John had been gripped by unease. He watched as people frantically chased high returns, yet his own greed and fear drove him to follow the crowd. Torn between the desire for easy, short-term gains and the fear of missing out, he ultimately abandoned his rational judgment. When the bubble burst, his investments evaporated almost instantly, pushing his company to the brink of bankruptcy. Many firms collapsed overnight, and his company was no exception, eventually declaring bankruptcy. This devastating loss was a harsh lesson. It taught John that short-term euphoria could blind even the most seasoned investors, and the price of chasing excessive profits was ruinous. From that moment on, he understood that true investment wisdom lay in patience and steadiness, and that risk management was the foundation of long-term survival.

However, it was the 2008 financial crisis that truly reshaped his outlook. The collapse of Lehman Brothers plunged global markets into chaos. This wasn't just a market crash; it was a reckoning for the entire financial system. John finally grasped the full danger posed by excessive leverage and the neglect of risk management.

During a meeting with his team, John addressed them gravely. "Risk isn't our enemy; it's a force we must control." He introduced a new risk assessment model, explaining its principles and how to apply them.

Phoenix Investment's strategy shifted away from solely pursuing short-term profits to building a robust portfolio with risk control as its core principle. John knew that only by respecting the market and its inherent risks could they maintain stability during future market fluctuations and uncover opportunities amidst crises.

From the Gulf War in 1990 to the Asian Financial Crisis of 1997, to the dot-com bubble in 2000, and the global financial crisis in 2008, John had witnessed each of these historic events and grown with every crisis. His investment philosophy had matured, and risk management became the cornerstone of both his life and career. No matter how the market fluctuated, John understood that what investors truly needed wasn't just the ability to profit, but a profound respect for and understanding of risk.

Reflection with Family and Friends

John sat in his office, gazing at the twinkling city lights outside his window, reflecting on his actions during the financial storm. Contemplating the dramatic shifts in the market, he realized that he needed more than just professional growth—he longed for inner peace and the support of his family. Wealth alone no longer held the same allure.

His wife, Mina, worked at an art museum and had a very different view of life. While she sought spiritual fulfillment and artistic enrichment, John had been consumed by the competition of the financial world for a long time. The crisis made him rethink their relationship and recognize both the diversity of life and the importance of family.

On a sunny afternoon in Central Park, John and Mina walked side by side, with leaves crunching beneath their feet. After a long silence, John took a deep breath and broke the stillness: "Mina, I used to think that pursuing financial success would bring everything—security, status, even happiness. But the financial crisis made me realize how wrong I was."

Mina watched him quietly, her eyes filled with understanding, waiting for him to continue.

"I thought that as long as I made enough money, our future would be secure. But in chasing wealth, I lost so many precious moments—moments that should have been ours." His voice cracked with regret as he whispered, "I neglected you, and I neglected our home."

Mina gently squeezed his hand and said softly, "John, I've always understood the pressure you've been under. But don't forget, you have this family—we've always been here for you."

In that moment, a warmth washed over John. He had thought that career success could bring him everything, but now he realized that the support of his family was an irreplaceable force in his life. "I finally understand that wealth isn't everything," he said quietly, his eyes filled with gratitude and reflection.

Beyond Mina, John also reached out to his parents back home. Hearing their familiar voices filled him with a long-lost sense of comfort. His parents reassured him, "Whatever you do, we support you. As long as you stay honest and kind, and stay grounded, you'll find your path."

These words, like a cool spring in the desert, soothed the restlessness in John's heart. As he continued to reflect, he invited several college friends to catch up and have an honest conversation. His friends shared their life journeys—some had started tech companies, while others had ventured into public welfare. Listening to their stories deeply inspired John.

"Money isn't the only measure of success," one old friend said. "The ability to truly make a difference in people's lives is the greatest achievement."

These words struck a chord with John. He began to reevaluate his life's goals, realizing that money was only a tool and that true success included social contribution and spiritual fulfillment. He started seeking more meaningful work, with a desire to use his influence to make a positive impact on the world.

As this inner transformation took place, John infused these ideals into Phoenix Investment's operations, driving the company to participate in more socially responsible projects and integrating ESG (Environmental, Social, and Governance) principles into its investment strategy. He believed finance should not only create wealth but also solve social and environmental problems.

After enduring the financial crisis, John experienced a profound shift in his worldview. No longer was he solely focused on material success; he sought deeper value and purpose. He thanked Mina for always being by his side, giving him unwavering support and encouragement. John knew that, with the strength of that love and support, the future would be brighter and more secure.

Future Opportunities

As markets gradually stabilized after the financial crisis, many companies began seeking opportunities to rebuild, while emerging industries rapidly rose to prominence. John clearly recognized this as an unprecedented era of transformation, with explosive growth awaiting in sectors ranging from new energy and technological innovation to infrastructure development.

Together with his team at Phoenix Investment, John began reassessing global investment opportunities. He no longer limited himself to short-term returns; instead, he turned his attention to enterprises capable of sustainable development and a positive global impact.

"John paced around the conference room. 'Everyone,' he began, 'we need to change our past investment strategy.' Instead of blindly pursuing short-term profits, we must look to the future and find companies that can change the world."

"What do you mean?" Katherine asked.

"I mean," John explained, "we should invest in companies dedicated to solving global problems, such as climate change, the energy crisis, and healthcare. While these companies might not yield high short-term returns, they possess enormous long-term potential and can make the world a better place."

Richard nodded in agreement: "You're right, John. We should not only create wealth for our clients but also contribute to society."

To achieve this goal, they actively began seeking companies focused on new energy, environmental technology, and medical innovation. John personally led the team to Silicon Valley to evaluate a startup developing highly efficient, environmentally friendly solar panels. In their laboratory, he witnessed young engineers breaking through technical bottlenecks and discussed the technology's potential in energy transition with the company's founders. This visit strengthened John's conviction that investing in companies leading future technological innovations was the right direction.

Meanwhile, John also turned his attention to medical technology, initiating collaboration with a European medical tech company. This company specialized in developing next-generation AI-assisted medical devices, showing particular promise in early cancer detection and telemedicine.

"Our goal is to make better healthcare accessible to more people," the company's CEO told John. "We hope our products can help people overcome illness and extend life."

"This is truly meaningful work," John responded. "I'm honored to be part of it."

John firmly believed this company's products would transform the future of healthcare. He decided to invest in the company, anticipating its contribution to human health.

These concrete actions not only reflected John's determination to reposition the company's development direction but also deepened his awareness of the inherent coexistence of risks and opportunities. Only with a forward-looking investment vision could one maintain a leading position in market competition.

In fact, John had already recognized the importance of ESG (Environmental, Social, and Governance) for future investments. He firmly believed that finance should not only create wealth but also shoulder the responsibility of solving global social and environmental issues. Therefore, John took the lead in incorporating ESG into Phoenix Investment's strategy, from supporting green energy projects to providing financing for small businesses in developing countries. These decisions stemmed from his profound insight and foresight into market trends.

As these strategic changes took effect, Phoenix Investment gradually reshaped its brand image and gained more trust from both the market and society. While other companies remained focused on short-term returns, John's forward-thinking vision led Phoenix Investment to stand out in the competition, becoming a market leader that balanced financial returns with social responsibility.

A New Beginning

In his personal life, John found himself embarking on an entirely new journey. No longer just a competitor in the financial markets, he had become a visionary leader. He learned to cherish the time spent with Mina and his family, making sure to put aside work every weekend for outings with them. Through his conversations with family and friends, John deeply realized the importance of balance and meaning in life, which helped him find harmony between his professional ambitions and his love for life.

"The future is no longer a frightening unknown," John said to Mina, pausing for a moment. "It's a journey filled with opportunities. We've weathered the storm, and because of it, we've become stronger and wiser."

Mina smiled and nodded, always supporting John's decisions. Their future was no longer reliant solely on the fluctuations of the market but was built on their shared beliefs and values.

However, just as everything seemed to settle into peace, an invitation from an international financial organization appeared on John's desk. The envelope bore a familiar insignia—an emblem of olive branches encircling a symbol representing power, stability, and control. "It was the mark of the **Global Monetary Strategic Alliance**, a shadowy organization that wielded immense influence within the global financial system."

John had heard whispers of this organization. It wielded immense influence in international finance, but its internal workings remained shrouded in secrecy. Some said it was a secret group that dictated global economic decisions, while others believed it to be merely an alliance of financial giants. Regardless of the truth, this invitation was far from an ordinary opportunity.

As John opened the letter, his heart surged with a mix of excitement and apprehension. The letter began:

"Dear John,

Your outstanding performance during the 2008 financial crisis not only helped countless companies recover but also demonstrated your profound insight into the global financial system. We have been closely following your achievements and believe you have the capability to participate in higher-level decision-making. Now, we sincerely invite you to join the **Global Monetary Strategic Alliance** to co-found a new organization and shape the next generation of global financial rules. We believe your wisdom and vision will have a lasting impact on the future development of the global economy.

This is an opportunity you cannot refuse, and we look forward to working with you to face the coming challenges and opportunities together."

These words resonated deeply with John. The letter not only acknowledged his past work but also expressed an expectation for him to influence the future of global finance. This wasn't merely a personal opportunity; it signified the chance to reshape the new order of global finance. The invitation meant he would ascend to the highest levels of economic decision-making, but hidden risks and burdens loomed large as well.

John's fingers brushed over the paper, filled with both anticipation and unease. Was this an open door to the future, or the start of a new storm? He stared at the letter, lost in thought. He knew this decision wouldn't just alter his personal destiny; it could very well change the trajectory of global finance.

But John did not rush to make a decision. He slowly closed the letter, placed it on the desk, and took a deep breath, his gaze shifting to the bustling Wall

Street outside, still filled with cars and people. The neon lights and hurried pedestrians came into view, evoking endless reflections on the world of finance.

"History doesn't repeat itself exactly," he whispered, his tone contemplative. "But stories often unfold in similar ways, and what remains eternal and unchanging is human nature."

The story wasn't over yet. A new chapter was just beginning.

About the Author

Harrison.H. is a writer and commentator specializing in global finance and economic trends, with a strong background in market analysis. His works blend cutting-edge financial knowledge with compelling narratives, guiding readers through the complexities of real-world economic shifts and international financial systems.

Through his writing, Harrison.H. delves into the intricate dynamics of financial systems and the pivotal human decisions that shape global economic trends, resonating deeply with readers. He aims to inspire readers to think critically about future economic developments and provide valuable insights.

Thank You for Reading!

Thank you for taking the time to read **The Age of Storms: John Reynolds' Financial Struggle**. I sincerely hope this story has inspired you or provided an enjoyable reading experience.

If you enjoyed this book, I kindly invite you to leave a review. Your feedback will not only help other readers discover this book but also encourage me to create even more exciting content in the future. Each positive review is a huge motivation for me!

Thank you again for your support, and I look forward to meeting you in my future works.

Sincerely,

Harrison.H.